BLACK POWER/
WHITE POWER
IN PUBLIC
EDUCATION

BLACK POWER/ WHITE POWER IN PUBLIC EDUCATION

Ralph Edwards and Charles V. Willie

 PRAEGER

Westport, Connecticut
London

Library of Congress Cataloging-in-Publication Data

Edwards, Ralph, 1930–
    Black power/white power in public education / Ralph Edwards and
Charles V. Willie.
        p. cm.
    Includes bibliographical references (p.) and index.
    ISBN 0–275–96201–6 (alk. paper)
        1. Politics and education—Massachusetts—Boston—Case studies.
2. Public schools—Massachusetts—Boston—Administration—Case
studies. 3. Wilson, Laval. 4. Afro-American school
superintendents—Case studies. I. Willie, Charles Vert, 1927– .
II. Title.
LC90.M4E39 1998
371.01'09744'61—dc21   97–32950

British Library Cataloguing in Publication Data is available.

Library of Congress Catalog Card Number: 97–32950
ISBN: 0–275–96201–6

First published in 1998

Praeger Publishers, 88 Post Road West, Westport, CT 06881
An imprint of Greenwood Publishing Group, Inc.

Printed in the United States of America

The paper used in this book complies with the
Permanent Paper Standard issued by the National
Information Standards Organization (Z39.48–1984).

10 9 8 7 6 5 4 3 2 1

Contents

Preface

This book is written from the perspective that education is a community affair. It is for the benefit of Black, Brown, and White people, poor and affluent people, females and males, and many other complementary categories of humankind.

Effective education is an experience that cannot be hoarded. Education is enhanced, not harmed, by increasing the number of people who participate in it. Thus, the full range of people in a local community should be studied if the goal is to understand public school policy formulation and implementation.

As a community enterprise, education is not exempt from the influences and forces of social power that activate community institutions toward the fulfillment of the goals of some people, away from fulfillment of the goals of others, or toward the fulfillment of goals that are mutually beneficial to all. This book, therefore, explores the dynamics of power among racial groups in the local community as they struggle for the fulfillment of their unique, joint goals and purposes through public education.

Case studies of two educational issues are analyzed in this book—one having to do with the hiring and firing of the first Black superintendent of schools in Boston, and the other having to do with the campaign to transform the Boston school committee from an elected to an appointed organization. These case studies are prototypes of educational issues faced by many communities. While each community, like each person, is an ecotype—unique and different from all other persons and communities—the power relationships manifested by community participants as they struggle to influence or force each other to behave in prescribed ways have similar and predictable patterns. Thus, the Boston experience is examined in depth for the edification of scholars, practitioners, policymakers, and parents with school-aged children in this community and in other communities.

Some population groups in a community have more power than other groups because of their numbers, resources, or organizational capacity. They are classified as dominant people of power. Populations with less power are designated as subdominants. However, both dominants and subdominants possess power. The latter, for example, possess the power of veto, or the ability to stop "business as usual" when they believe that their fundamental interests are not being well served.

These descriptions enable us to avoid the trap of essentialism, wherein one group in the community, such as Whites, is viewed as all-powerful always while others, like ethnic minorities, are seen as having no power at all. Moreover, according to this definition, dominant status is not necessarily permanent. A group that achieves dominance in one period during a community's history may be subdominant in another. Dominance, in this view, is shaped by changing historical circumstances and by the particular situation under consideration.

All of this is to say that the analysis of educational issues within the context of community should not assume that the appropriate course of action is that manifested by the prevailing population group or the dominant people of power. Always, there are contending power groups in the community with valid goals that may differ. The task of public administrators and educational policymakers is to reconcile the interests of disparate community groups into a complementary whole, with neither dominants always winning nor subdominants always losing.

This book describes how dominant and subdominant population groups win and lose in the community power game pertaining to public education. We deliberately selected issues to analyze that involved the interests of Blacks so that we and our readers could examine and understand race relations within the context of community power relations. Seldom do studies of community power examine in depth the actions of subdominants. This study tries to correct for this frequent omission.

The conclusions emerging from this study contribute to accumulated knowledge in community organization, community development, and community decision making and to the fields that analyze these, such as sociology and social work, political science, and public administration. Findings should be of special interest to practitioners and policymakers in public education, such as superintendents, other system-wide administrators and school board members. Finally, the discussions in this book may be helpful to scholars concerned with policy analysis and to community activists concerned with social change.

We acknowledge with appreciation the Ford Foundation and the Maurice Falk Medical Fund for grants to Ralph Edwards and Boston College and to Charles Willie and Harvard University for support of this study. The findings and conclusions are those of the authors and do not necessarily reflect the official policies of the granting or sponsoring organizations. Also, we are grateful for the excellent work of our research assistants, Lisa Gonsalves of the University of Massachusetts at Boston for assistance in writing chapter 3, and Donna Jones of Harvard University for assistance in writing chapter 2, and for the expert editing and editorial advice offered by David Breakstone. Kathleen George was the project secretary and administrative assistant and was most skillful in shepherding it to a timely closure.

1. _____ Introduction: The Efficacy of Local Community Action

To Massachusetts Congressman Thomas P. O'Neill, Jr., former Speaker of the U.S. House of Representatives, is attributed the saying that all politics are local. However, it was Martin Luther King, Jr. by way of the Civil Rights Movement who demonstrated that this is so.

Local grassroots campaigns led by King in Montgomery, Birmingham, Selma, St. Augustine, Chicago, and elsewhere were effective. In Montgomery, for example, the 1955 boycott of the city buses by Blacks led to a U.S. Supreme Court decision in 1956 that declared racially segregated seating on buses unconstitutional. When word of that decision reached Montgomery, "a mass meeting was . . . scheduled that evening to give the people final instructions before returning to the buses the following day" (King 1958:147). Thus, effective local community organization prepared the people to seize and follow-up on their opportunity to receive desegregated city bus service. This local opportunity had national significance. To experience transportation desegregation in Montgomery, Blacks did not have to wait ten years or more as some Black communities did to experience court-ordered school desegregation. Local communities that had to wait many years for the fulfillment of the promise of school desegregation often were not organized to seize their court-ordered victory.

In 1960 Greensboro, North Carolina, was the setting where four first-year Black college students took seats at a lunch counter in a Woolworth's store that served lunch to White people only. The students were refused service, but they refused to move. "In the next two weeks," according to Zinn, "sit-ins spread to fifteen cities in five southern states" (Zinn 1995:444). Thus, from this and other local actions the direct-action phase of the Civil Rights Movement began. In the end, legislation such as the Civil Rights Act of 1964, the Voting Rights Act of 1965, and the Fair Housing Act of 1968 was enacted largely because of local demonstrations. Local action had national consequences.

We are now one generation or more beyond the era of local, grass-roots demonstrations. Yet Blacks and other people of color are still struggling to obtain social justices. This study examines the action strategies used by Blacks and Whites at the local level today as the struggle continues.

Manuel Castells, author of *The City and the Grassroots*, reports that "After the end of collective violent protest of the American inner cities in the 1960s, a steady flow of community organizations and neighborhood groups demanding public services quietly irrigated the country's geography through the 1970s" (Castells 1983:328). Having analyzed contemporary urban movements all over the world, Castells concludes that genuine social change occurs only when those movements reflect three basic principles of community organization: (1) they self-identify as citizen movements operating under the rubric of self-determination, (2) they are locally based and territorially defined, and (3) they tend to mobilize around three major goals—collective consumption, cultural identity, and political self-management (Castells 1983:328). The absence of any one of these three principles may render the movement less effective. The demonstrations led by Martin Luther King, Jr. brought together all of these themes.

In this study, we identify the presence or absence of these principles in specific community efforts by African Americans in Boston during the post–civil rights era. By focusing on a single city, we emphasize the contextual circumstances of community leadership. Among the significant issues emerging from these circumstances are the following:

- The presence or absence of critical mass in the size of a challenge-group and how it facilitates or impedes effective community action.
- The assets and liabilities of coalition politics.
- The values of consensus versus bureaucratic decision making and their interrelationships.

- The relative merits of conflict and cooperation as strategies for social action.
- The manner in which pluralistic populations harmonize or fail to harmonize their separate political interests.

THE BOSTON CONTEXT

Changing circumstances in Boston during the 1960s that led to a court order to desegregate the city's schools have had on-going effects into the 1990s and beyond. First, in 1961, the National Association for the Advancement of Colored People (NAACP) asked the Massachusetts Commission Against Discrimination (MCAD) to conduct a study of discrimination in school assignments. When the MCAD declared there was no discrimination, the NAACP conducted its own study and charged Boston with operating segregated schools. The Congress of Racial Equality (CORE) issued a similar report and also charged that educational facilities in Boston were unequal for Black students. After the Boston School Committee claimed there was no discrimination, the Black community boycotted the Boston schools in June 1963, and in February 1964. As a result of these activities the Massachusetts State Board of Education launched a study that found that Boston schools were, in fact, racially imbalanced.

The resistance of the Boston School Committee stimulated many African Americans to become more politically active. They solicited support from suburban areas, the state legislature, and the governor. Eventually, the NAACP enlisted support from the Harvard Center of Law and Education and filed a complaint in the U.S. District Court in 1972. In 1974, the court in the case of *Morgan versus Hennigan*, found the Boston School Committee guilty of operating a dual school system that discriminated against Black children (Smith 1978:25–113). This victory emboldened Blacks in Boston to confront other injustices and strengthened their participation in local and state political systems.

Looking back at the school desegregation struggle, one should remember that it importantly set the stage for the cases described in this study. We briefly review that period to better understand the background out of which the cases analyzed in this book eventually developed.

The ugly nature of the resistance to school desegregation in Boston brought opprobrium to the city. It also forced the U.S. District Court into an uncharacteristically close supervisory role over Boston's public schools. Violence, although not widespread, became the immediate and most indelible response in 1974 to the first stage (Phase I) of the court's desegregation plan. (See, for example, Lucas 1985.)

Phase I was not a remedy the court itself designed, but a partial plan the State Education Department had developed in response to desegregation mandates of the state judiciary. The state plan, among other things, called for the busing of students by pairing a neighborhood like Roxbury, a predominantly Black area, with South Boston, a White section of the city, where signs of hostility toward Blacks had already been noted (Lucas 1985). This plan affected about 40 percent of all Boston students. Judge W. Arthur Garrity, Jr. decided to employ the state's plan as Phase I of his desegregation plan, since the Boston School Committee refused to develop a plan. Meanwhile the court developed its own permanent plan that was implemented in Phase II, beginning with the 1975–76 school year.

On September 12, 1974, when the new school year began, Black students arriving by bus at South Boston High School were met by hostile crowds screaming racial insults. Later in the day, when the students were attempting to leave, bottles and rocks were thrown at them, and some were injured (Lucas 1985). That evening, television coverage sent pictures of these events across the nation. In following days, other racial incidents occurred and these, too, were reported nationally by the media. By October, the violence had reached a point where the governor felt compelled to call in the National Guard to maintain order (Lucas 1985).

Phase II, the permanent plan issued May 10, 1975, also began with episodes of violence. This further contributed to the general picture of violent racial conflict that became the backdrop to Boston's school desegregation struggle. Perhaps the most enduring symbol of that period is a prize-winning 1976 photograph that shows a White youth in front of Boston's City Hall attempting to spear a Black man with an American flag (Lucas 1985). The Black man was a lawyer on his way to meet with the mayor; the youth belonged to a group of White high school students who had just met with City Council members concerning the school desegregation crisis. The significance of all of this to our case studies is that these events became a serious, lasting embarrassment to the city's reputation and pride. Boston, after all, was the capital of a commonwealth with a long tradition of liberalism: it was in Massachusetts that the abolitionist movement is alleged to have begun; Massachusetts was the home of the liberal Kennedys; the state had sent Edward Brooke, the first Black since Reconstruction, to the U.S. Senate. Boston would, in time, want to show that what had happened during the desegregation of its schools did not, or at least no longer, represented its true character as a city.

However, during the desegregation period White elected officials, in general, and School Committee members, in particular, opted to defy the law (Lucas 1985). The popular course for them was to blame the court and Judge Garrity for a situation that they and many of their White constituents deeply resented. As elected officials, they chose constituency demands over their obligation to uphold the law. They were not invisible or neutral in the matter, thus displaying the critical failure of leadership for which many observers have held them responsible. Rather, they were active leaders of opposition to the court's orders, and several were rewarded for their leadership by election or reelection to public office.

Over time, however, the court's will prevailed: appeals of verdicts and court orders were heard by higher courts and consistently rejected; defiant public officials were handled gingerly by the judge who, instead of imprisoning them and possibly turning them into martyrs, outwaited them while moving ever more deeply into the daily operation of the schools. Gradually, and out of conflict, a grudging sense of order was restored. This, in turn, permitted some measure of rational assessment concerning the damage that had been done.

Kevin White was Boston's mayor throughout most of the school desegregation struggle. A pluralist politician in an almost "classical" Boston mold, he was confronted by this struggle with one of pluralism's worst dilemmas: a conflict between strong constituent demands and the law. His response was to cast doubt on the law and the wisdom of the court for its orders, while portraying himself as powerless to do anything about desegregation. Behind the scenes, however, White attempted to negotiate with both sides of the desegregation dispute, particularly with anti-busing forces, since they posed the greatest threat to public order. But, of course, he satisfied neither. He once characterized himself as a demolitions expert trying to defuse a bomb that if done incorrectly could turn him into a political paraplegic.

Despite a tumultuous, crisis-strewn tenure, White was reelected in 1979 to an unprecedented fourth consecutive term as mayor. In his 1979 inaugural speech, White called for an end to racial tensions, returning to the theme of reconciliation with which he had begun his mayoralty.

But while White's pursuit of this theme during his final term was mostly rhetorical, his successor, Raymond Flynn, made it a serious priority of his administration. As a state representative from South Boston, Flynn was a staunch opponent of busing and school desegregation. But, as mayor, he, too, saw the need to heal the city's wounds.

All told, Judge Garrity issued over four hundred separate court orders in the *Morgan* case. This large number was prompted by the reluctance of school officials to carry out responsibilities connected with the court's desegregation plans that were not explicitly spelled out by the court. The court's orders, therefore, became more and more specific, which then resulted in the gradual displacement of the School Department's administrative authority. As the situation became more stable, however, the court began to look forward to withdrawing from the case. Beginning in May 1981, it initiated a consent decree process that culminated on December 23, 1982, with a final disengagement plan.

Reflecting Doug McAdam's model, the "realignment of political forces" in post–civil rights Boston was importantly aided by the Federal Court's desegregation role. That role provided crucial help in changing "existing political arrangement," thus affording Blacks "greater leverage with which to advance their interests" (McAdams 1982:39).

The cases cited in this study depict how Blacks in Boston did or did not use this leverage in two vital instances relating to public education. In the first, we examine the selection in 1985 of Laval Wilson, Boston's first African American superintendent of schools and the process that resulted in his dismissal in 1990. In the second case, we examine how Boston's thirteen–member elected School Committee was transformed in 1991 to a seven–person school board appointed by the mayor.

CONCEPTS AND PRINCIPLES

As the cases in this volume will illustrate, the post–civil rights endeavors of African Americans to improve their social conditions continue to be a struggle for power. Consequently, certain basic premises of "power-structure" research that comprised some of the earlier

Black leadership studies retain their relevance. Among the best known of earlier studies are Hunter's (1953) examination of Atlanta's Black leadership and his follow-up study published in 1980, Pfautz's 1962 study of Providence, Rhode Island, and Barth and Abu-Laban's (1959) study of Seattle, Washington.

These and other studies of the "power-structure" genre proceed from the premise that interaction between the structural components of a community are mediated by a process phenomenon called power. Power, in turn, may be defined as the capacity of an individual or group to force or influence others to behave in a prescribed manner. Ultimately, all relationships and social processes in the human community are mediated by power, according to this view. Thus, all interactions among individuals, groups, and other collectivities within a community are essentially power relations.

Moreover, it is important to note, that all people have power, subdominants as well as dominants. Both groups, for example, possess veto power—the capacity to interfere with and stop normal actions or "business as usual." But the capacity to implement alternative action strategies (through the process of legislation, for example) is a prerogative limited to dominant people of power. Thus, subdominants (people with less power) must influence dominants to adopt their agenda in order to achieve effective community action. One way for them to do this is to establish coalitions or make common cause with other subdominants and thereby become collective dominants themselves. Indeed, coalition building to produce political majorities is fundamental to the pluralist bargaining process that some depict as axiomatic to political democracy (see, for example, Dahl 1961; Banfield 1961; Peterson 1976). Regardless of the approach to goal achievement that dominants and subdominants employ, "power and its differential distribution is the medium that links [micro-social] units within a [macro social] system" (Willie 1994:90). Without power, there is no purposeful community action.

The above summation of "power-structure" research philosophy identifies the fundamental link between our study and that particular research genre. We, too, seek to examine dominant and subdominant power relationships to better understand how pluralistic and disparate groups interact while seeking to achieve common community goals. Too often, however, the internal dynamics of subdominant people of power are not addressed in power structure analyses. We especially encounter this error in studies of community power structure.

Floyd Hunter, for example, defined power as "the ability of [people] to move goods and services toward goals designated by persons of authority" (1953:58). This definition recognizes only dominants as having the capacity "to move goods and services," and fails to take into consideration subdominants who may not have the capacity "to move goods and services" but who do have the capacity to stop their movement. The Montgomery bus boycott was a dramatic demonstration of veto power by subdominants (King 1958).

Indeed, under Martin Luther King, Jr.'s leadership, Montgomery introduced the disciplined, nonviolent use of a veto strategy by African Americans that led directly to the Civil Rights Movement. Other movements, such as the Peace Movement and the Women's Movement, later copied this strategy with notable success. This was the era of protest politics whose success led to legislation (e.g., the Civil Rights Act of 1964 and Voting Rights Act of 1965) which, among other things, dramatically increased the number of Black elected officials. This particular outcome, as Adolph Reed, Jr. points out, "altered the strategic bases of Black political activity by creating [a] division of labor in which political officials have primary responsibility for conversion of Black concerns into legitimate policy agenda items" (1986:3).

If Black insurgency has faded during the post–civil rights era, one could say that protest politics has been largely diffused by its own success at gaining access to mainstream public policy arenas. However, the leadership implications of this reality, particularly at the local level, are seldom systematically examined. Therefore, we have too little knowledge about how modern Black leadership is, in fact, formed and how it reaches decisions within the current context of increased Black elected representation. Citing Hunter again (mainly because his is the best known of the earlier Black leadership studies), he concludes that "the pattern of leadership within the [African American] community follows rather closely the pattern of the larger community" (1953:114). This conclusion, reached before the Montgomery Bus Boycott, is disconfirmed in our own research. Hunter probably arrived at this conclusion because he used the same method to identify leaders in the Black community that he used to identify those in the White community. For example, his field interviewers began with this question, "Who is the top leader in the community?" (Hunter 1953:27).

This question assumed that community decision making is always structured in bureaucratic, hierarchical, and vertical ways. Our studies of community leadership among African Americans who are subdominant people of power indicate that their decision making is achieved more through consensual, horizontal interactions. Among subdominants, there may or may not be a top leader; usually, there are multiple leaders.

Given the post–civil rights conditions in Black communities, particularly urban Black communities, one also wonders how African Americans of different social classes can find common ground for community action as they did in the Montgomery situation.

We know that social class cleavages within Black communities have importantly widened in the post–civil rights era. For example, Lusane, in an important study, *African Americans at the Crossroads: The Restructuring of Black Leadership and the 1992 Elections*, reports that the proportion of Black families with annual incomes over $35,000 increased from 15.7 percent to 21.1 percent between 1970 and 1986 respectively, while the proportion earning less than $10,000 annually during that same period also increased from 26.6 percent to 30.2 percent in those same years. Indeed, the Black poverty rate of 32 percent, Lusane reports, is higher than for other major ethnic groups, such as Hispanics (28.7%), Asians (13.2%), and Whites (11.3%) (Lusane 1994:4). Andrew Billingsley writes about the decline in the Black working class, stating that Black industrial employment fell much faster than overall employment in the manufacturing sector (Billingsley 1992:133, 138, 139). And William Julius Wilson reports that "a neighborhood with a paucity of regularly employed families. . . experiences social isolation" (1987:59).

African American poverty is most obvious in urban areas where 81 percent of Black Americans now reside. Lusane observes that "the unleashing of the voting potential of Blacks and the concentration of Blacks in critical urban centers [have become] the foundations on which new Black leadership would emerge" (1994: 21). Given the poverty of Blacks in urban centers, however, one wonders how this leadership's formation, agendas, and actual performance might be affected by the deepening divisions of social class. And, although Black elected officials now have, in Adolph Reed Jr.'s words, "primary responsibility for conversion of Black concerns into legitimate public policy agenda items" (1986:3), we need to know how well this has been accomplished at the local level.

We intend to analyze who actually provides the critical leadership for local African American communities, elected or nonelected individuals. These and other questions pertaining to internal elements of local, African American leadership have yet to be satisfactorily answered. The answers, moreover, must be balanced with updated understandings of post–civil rights urban power structures and how these are manifested in the Black community and between Black and other communities. As times have changed, these power structures, too, have adapted to meet new municipal challenges. The dominant people of power in municipal power structures, however, continue to rely heavily upon the age-old strategy of "divide and conquer," and we need to learn how well Blacks have countered this strategy during the post–civil rights era.

New empirical studies are needed. Earlier ones, as noted, were methodologically flawed and, in any case, are now seriously dated. Indeed, the most extensive review of Black leadership literature to date, Robert Smith's *Black Leadership: A Survey of Theory and Research* (1982), is more than a decade old. Smith's most recent study, *We Have No Leaders*, was published in 1996. However, it focuses largely on Black leadership at the national level.

While criticizing case study methodology as yielding non-generalizable results, Smith nonetheless concludes that "there are few studies of the new [post–civil rights] Black leadership which are of the depth and sophistication of studies pertaining to the old Negro leadership" (Smith 1982:90). He also declares that new "research on the power-structure of the Black community—both nationally and locally—should be undertaken" (Smith 1982:99). The case studies in this volume are intended to help meet this need.

RESEARCH ISSUES AND HYPOTHESES

This study was conceptualized as an examination of social structures and processes in the Black community. It is an investigation of Black leadership and decision making and the responses of Whites. It is not an assessment of the personalities, motives, and adaptations of individuals. Our analysis deals with the dynamics of group and institutional changes and not with changes in personal attitudes. While we recognize and accept the fact that individual orientations, attitudes, and motivations may influence social organization, our purpose in undertaking this study is to discover how community structures and processes limit or facilitate the choices of individuals and influence people to take action either consistent or inconsistent with their group interests.

As stated by Peter Blau, "structural conditions influence processes of social association" and it may be assumed that "every group in society is related to other groups" (1977:19). This is a study of how the Black community in Boston as a collectivity differentiates itself from other collectivities—how it determines what is the self-interest of Blacks as a collectivity, and also how it establishes linkages with other collectivities necessary for fulfilling the self-interest of African Americans. Specifically, this is a study of differentiation, integration, and collaboration. To work with others, a group or collectivity must have a sense of its own significance and what it needs and what it has to offer. Yet, in the process of developing an appreciation of its own strengths, a group or collectivity comes to understand in a profound way its limitations, weaknesses, and need for others. Alone, we are incomplete: none is self-sufficient. The challenge of living in community is to learn how to be oneself and, simultaneously, to be part of a group.

James Blackwell and Philip Hart discovered in a study of Black men and women in Atlanta, Boston, Cleveland, Houston, and Los Angeles during the late 1970s and early 1980s, that the urgent concerns of Blacks in order of descending significance were the following: (1) better economic conditions, (2) better education, (3) crime and drug abuse, (4) equal justice, (5) better housing, (6) political power, (7) better public service, and (8) police brutality (Blackwell and Hart 1982:53). To deal with these concerns, the Black community must formulate its own expectations and action plans regarding what is just and fair and must also decide how to work with others for mutual fulfillment.

Blackwell and Hart found that the rank order of the pressing community concerns varied in the Black community and had different rank-orders by age, gender, level of education, income, and occupation (1982:66–73). These findings indicate that achieving unity of expectation and action within this community is a challenging task. Nevertheless, our study shows that it is achievable. We will examine how the Black community in Boston attempts to create unity despite its diversity.

Of the social problems faced by African Americans, Blackwell and Hart state that "many. . . are structural in nature; some are community specific." They report that "a strong belief is prevalent [among some individuals] in the Black community that their fate is, unfortunately, in the hands of others, especially within a White power structure" (Blackwell and Hart 1982:74). We will explore how the Black community in Boston collaborates with others, including the White power structure, on whom their fate, in part, may depend, even as the fate of Whites, in part, depends on the actions of people of color.

The notion of working with others, especially with those holding opposing views, is always a challenge. Defining one's own interests while, at the same time, working with others because of the absence of self-sufficiency is a problem that has not been solved effectively by most collectivities of subdominant people of power. Mulana Karenga is emphatic in his statement that "there is. . . no substitute for the structural capacity to define, defend and develop one's interest" (Karenga 1993:340). Yet, Blackwell and Hart observe that some Blacks believe that their fate is in the hands of others because they themselves lack the resources or authority to change their conditions. These two statements suggest that the establishment of coalitions may be necessary to achieve some of the goals of the Black community. Karenga, however, would approach coalitions cautiously. His observation is that "Blacks have assumed too much about their relationship with their more powerful coalition partners and left themselves vulnerable to joint actions not mutually beneficial" (Karenga 1993:338). Seeming to acknowledge that coalitions may sometimes be necessary, Karenga gives advice on how the less powerful partner can achieve a measure of protection. He states that the subdominant population can unite with other less powerful partners in coalition to increase power (Karenga 1993:339).

We will examine how the Black community in Boston tries to bring about a more egalitarian decision-making structure and the methods and techniques used to participate in it. Particular attention will be given to whether the Boston Black community relies on coalition building, political patronage, the power of voluntary associations, or other strategies to reduce inequality. We also examine whether Boston

Blacks favor centralization or decentralization and local control as an approach to gaining their fair share of power.

Finally, we will analyze the techniques used by members of the Boston Black community to resist or overcome the harmful actions of others. Are resistance efforts among Boston Blacks spontaneous or planned? Do Blacks in Boston believe in retribution—an eye for an eye? Do they fight fire with fire, which is the symmetrical way of dealing with adversity? Or do they follow an asymmetrical approach of meeting physical force with soul force, as the Black community did in the Montgomery Bus Boycott?

Galbraith has stated it as a rule that "almost any manifestation of power will induce an opposite. . . . manifestation of power." For example, "any effort to bend people to submission will encounter in some form an effort to resist that submission" (Galbraith 1983:74). He describes the symmetry between the sources of power and the countervailing response as having a certain classic clarity in many areas (Galbraith 1983:77). Although Galbraith calls symmetry in the use of power "the rule," he acknowledges that "there have been striking examples in history of countering or countervailing power that have depended for their effectiveness on their asymmetry" (Galbraith 1983:79). Martin Luther King, Jr. and Mahatma Gandhi are mentioned as leaders of subdominant people of power who effectively broke the accepted and accustomed dialectic of power (Galbraith 1983:80) and won through asymmetrical action.

We intend to demonstrate the conditions under which one or another approach is more efficacious in community decision making, and the circumstances and conditions under which a specific action strategy is likely to be more dramatically effective for subdominant people.

RESEARCH METHODS

In the 1960s, the Ford Foundation made grants to several universities to support case studies of how metropolitan communities solve their problems and provide governmental services. *Decisions in Syracuse* was one of the first books published from this research (Martin and Munger et al. 1961). We decided to adopt the case method of this study for our study of Black leadership in the Boston metropolitan area. The case method is a useful way to study community organizations, as Samuel Stouffer, a brilliant methodologist in statistical analysis, demonstrated in his doctoral dissertation submitted to the University of Chicago. He advocated use of the case method not only because it can obtain some results that are similar to those obtained by way of quantitative analysis but also because it "suggest[s] connecting links in processes which may elude the statistician" (Stouffer 1980:11 of abstract).

Until their study was published, Martin, Munger, and their colleagues discovered that "there [had] been no serious effort to relate the patterns of influence within the community to the institutional structures of the community government" (Martin and Munger et al. 1961:13). We plan to overcome this omission in our Boston study of Black leadership.

We also plan to examine the decision-making structure of the Black community to determine if it is monolithic or polylithic. A polylithic community is one in which power is shared among competitive social groups (Martin and Munger et al. 1961:10–11). Our hypothesis is that the Black power structure in the Boston community is probably more polylithic than monolithic.

We, like the Syracuse researchers, focus not on Black individuals who have the reputation of being community leaders but instead on the various decisions that are made, who is involved, and how individuals, groups, organizations, and associations are involved (Martin and Munger et al. 1961:4). In effect, we identify the roles involved in the exercise of community power (Martin and Munger et al. 1961:323).

A significant finding of the Syracuse study is that "separate clusters of decision areas exist, each with its own distinct group of participants." We will examine the Boston community to determine if this is so among Blacks.

After reviewing news reports and talking with many informants, we identified six issues, beginning with the mayoral election in 1983, which was the first time that a Black candidate, Mel King, became a serious challenger for the office of mayor of Boston. We sent letters to ninety-six Black individuals who had been active in the community's affairs: politicians, youth service workers, social service agency administrators, settlement house executives, voluntary association leaders, officers of civil rights organizations, staff of legal aid services, ministers of churches, health and welfare counselors and care givers, educators in public schools and private schools, educators in higher education institutions, and leaders of neighborhood associations. These letters requested that the issues identified should be scrutinized to determine if they were significant in the life of the Black community of Boston; informants also were requested to rank the issues indicating their relative importance. We asked respondents to suggest other issues of importance to Boston's Black community that might not have been listed.

Of the total number of Black individuals contacted, approximately forty responded either by mail or to follow-up telephone calls. Black community informants ranked the six issues selected in the following order of importance: the Mel King mayoral race of 1983 was the most important, Dianne Wilkerson's successful run for a seat in the Senate of the Commonwealth of Massachusetts was ranked second. The issue of an appointed versus an elected school committee was ranked third followed by the housing discrimination court case initiated by the NAACP against the Boston Housing Authority. Fifth was the hiring and firing of the first Black superintendent of schools in Boston. Ranked last was the proposal to carve out of Boston a separate city of Black people to be called Mandela.

Most informants agreed that these were important issues in the Black community. However, a few named additional issues such as policing and public safety in the Black community, "red lining" and discriminatory lending practices by banks in Boston, economic development in the Black community, decreasing support for health and social welfare services in the Black community, the hiring of the first Black woman superintendent of schools in Boston, and the Bruce Bolling candidacy for mayor of Boston in 1993. Bolling is Black and had served on the City Council.

The issues that we identified may be classified as political and educational. Additional issues mentioned by Black community informants may be classified as political, educational, as well as economic. Of the different kinds of issues discussed, political issues were most frequently mentioned by Black informants.

We plan to analyze the political and economic issues in separate documents. This book is devoted to an analysis of two significant educational issues. However, these educational issues have important political implications. The two case studies analyzed in this book are: (a) the hiring and firing of the first Black Superintendent of Schools in

Boston, and (b) how Boston's elected School Committee was changed to a mayorally appointed board.

REFERENCES

Banfield, E. 1961. *Political Influence*. New York: The Free Press.

Barth, E. and B. Abu-Laban. 1959. "Power Structure in the Negro Subcommunity." *American Sociological Review* 24, pp. 69–76.

Billingsley, A. 1992. *Climbing Jacob's Ladder*. New York: Simon and Schuster.

Blackwell, J. and P. Hart. 1982. *Cities, Suburbs and Blacks*. Dix Hills, NY: General Hall.

Blau, Peter. 1977. *Inequality and Heterogeneity*. New York: The Free Press.

Castells, Manuel. 1983. *The City and the Grassroots*. Berkeley, CA: University of California Press.

Dahl, R. 1961. *Who Governs?* New Haven, CT: Yale University Press.

Galbraith, J. K. 1983. *The Anatomy of Power*. Boston: Houghton-Mifflin.

Hunter, Floyd. 1953. *Community Power Structure*. Chapel Hill, NC: University of North Carolina.

Karenga, Mulana. 1993. *Introduction to Black Studies*. 2nd ed. Los Angeles, CA: University of Sankore Press.

King, Martin Luther, Jr. 1958. *Stride Toward Freedom*. New York: Harper and Row.

Lucas, J. Anthony. 1985. *Common Ground*. New York: Alfred A. Knopf.

Lusane, Clarence. 1994. *African Americans at the Crossroads: The Restructuring of Black Leadership and the 1992 Elections*. Boston: South End Press.

McAdams, Doug. 1982. *Political Process and the Development of Black Insurgency 1930–1970*. Chicago: University of Chicago Press.

Martin, Roscoe C., Frank J. Munger and others. 1961. *Decisions in Syracuse*. Bloomington: Indiana University Press (re-issued in 1965 by Doubleday and Company).

Morgan vs. Hennigan, 379 F/ Supp. 410 (D. Mass. 1974), *aff'd sub nom. Morgan v. Kerrigan*, 509 F. 2d 580 (1st Cir. 1974), *cert. denied*, 421 U.S. 963 (1975).

Peterson, P. 1976. *Politics Chicago Style*. Chicago: University of Chicago Press.

Pfautz, H. 1962. "The Power Structure of the Negro Subcommunity: A Case Study and Comparative View." *Phylon* (Summer), pp. 156–66.

Reed, Adolph J., Jr., 1986. *The Jesse Jackson Phenomenon*. New Haven, CT: Yale University Press.

Smith, Ralph R. 1978. "Two Centuries and Twenty-Four Months: A Chronicle of the Struggle to Desegregate the Boston Public Schools." In Howard I. Kalodner and James F. Fishman (eds.), *Limits of Justice*. Pp. 25–113. Cambridge, MA: Ballinger.

Smith, Robert. 1982. *Black Leadership: A Survey of Theory and Research*. Washington, DC: Howard University Press.

Smith, Robert. 1996. *We Have No Leaders*. Albany, NY: State University of New York Press.

Stouffer, Samuel. 1980. *An Experimental Comparison of Statistical and Case History Methods of Attitude Research*. New York: Arno Press. (Originally presented as a dissertation to the University of Chicago in 1930 for the Ph.D. degree in sociology.)

Willie, Charles V. 1994. *Theories of Human Social Action*. Dix Hills, NY: General Hall.

Wilson, William Julius. 1987. *The Truly Disadvantaged*. Chicago: University of Chicago Press.

Zinn, Howard. 1995. *A People's History of the United States—1492–Present*. New York: Harper Perennial.

2. _____ The Hiring and Firing of Laval Wilson, Boston's First African American Superintendent of Schools

Prior to Laval Wilson, Robert Spillane had been superintendent of Boston's public schools. At the end of June 1985, with the School Committee's approval, he left his position to accept the superintendency in Fairfax County, Virginia. Joseph McDonough, a deputy superintendent, was chosen by the committee to serve as interim superintendent until July 31, 1985.

The initial significance of Spillane's appointment was that he was an "outsider." Spillane had previously held superintendencies in New York and New Jersey. Given the tradition within which Boston's schools functioned, for an outsider to become superintendent was no small accomplishment. Boston's was a deeply inbred school system, reflecting at every level the local Irish-Catholic hegemony that had prevailed in the city for almost a half-century. An impression of this condition just prior to the school desegregation struggle is gained from the following description of the School Department's central headquarters:

At 15 Beacon, where they are crammed into drab green cubicles with their secretaries and mimeograph machines, the McDonough's still speak mainly to the O'Leary's, the Casey's and the Hogan's, directing the world of 68 Sullivans, 61 Murphy's, 21 Lynches, 18 Kelleys, 14 Kelly's, 25 Walshes, 30 O'Briens, 40 McCarthy's, 22 Doherty's, 21 McLaughlin's, and

This chapter was written with the assistance of Donna Jones.

some 3700 other teachers and administrators, most of whom are Irish. (Schrag 1967: 51)

There was, beyond ethnic homogeneity, a commonality of social class and educational background among them. Most were lower middle class and had attended the same schools through college. The colleges included Boston College, Boston State, Regis, and Emmanuel. Boston College, especially, had been the training ground for the school system's central administration staff. In the late 1960s according to Schrag,

All but one member of the Board of Superintendents, the senior staff of the system, [were] graduates of Boston College, all [had] risen through the ranks and [had] been in the system for more than three decades, all [were] well over 50 years old, all [were] Catholics, and (except for the superintendent), all [were] Irishmen. (1967:55)

In the School Department, they had come together in the manner of an extended family. A network of informal relations provided job security and played a more important role than the civil service in gaining professional advancement. Members of this network linked themselves selectively with individual members of the School Committee who, in exchange for information and loyalty, provided additional support and sponsored promotion within the system (Schrag 1967).

Educationally, this was not an environment in which innovation could flourish. On the contrary, it promoted the status quo, a condition that Schrag depicted as "From the top to somewhere near the very bottom, the Boston system is steeped in conservative ideas and traditional practices, in a patronizing outlook, and in subtle prejudice. Its leaders look upon themselves as caretakers" (1967:72).

This is the system Spillane inherited and the one whose conservatism, inbreeding, and outright racism had precipitated the *Morgan* case in 1974. By the early 1980s, the system's basic internal character had still not changed. Nevertheless, by 1985 change had been imposed upon it, both by the federal court and by events themselves.

By issuing over four-hundred court orders to force compliance with the law, the federal court had assumed de facto control of Boston's public schools. The only way the city could regain control was by complying with both the letter and the spirit of the court's mandates. By 1985, this had not only become abundantly clear to city officials, but regaining control of the school system had become a municipal priority. Thus, Raymond Flynn, who became mayor in 1983 and who, as a state legislator had himself opposed the court's presence, took the lead in creating a climate that would enhance accomplishing this goal. Such a climate might also help neutralize the racist image the city had incurred as a consequence of the desegregation struggle.

By this time Boston's public school population had become mostly non-White. The population in Boston dropped from 801,000 in 1950 to 574,000 in 1990 for a net decrease of 227,000 or 28 percent. The drop in population is often attributed to court-ordered school desegregation. However, our analysis shows that the largest proportional drop in population during this forty-year period occurred before school desegregation, between 1950 and 1970. Between 1970 and 1990, which may be classified as the decades of desegregation litigation, only 30 percent of the total decrease in population had occurred (U.S. Bureau of the Census 1960, 1994).

The decade of the 1970s was turbulent in Boston. Desegregation was ordered by the court and was violently resisted in some communities. Yet, Boston's population dropped by only 12 percent. This proportion parallels the 13 percent reduction that occurred between 1950 and 1960, years before the words "desegregation" and "forced busing" were widely used in public discourse. It would appear, therefore, that school desegregation is not the major cause of Boston's decreasing population since 1950, as claimed by some analysts.

Three phenomena that seem to be associated with the reduction of Whites in large urban populations since 1950 are the declining birthrate, an increasing popularity of suburban living since the end of World War II, and the increasing proportion of people of color in urban areas. The White birthrate per 1,000 population in the United States has decreased from 24.1 in 1950 to 15.5 in 1990. This represents a 38 percent decline. A study of population decreases during a single decade in four cities—Atlanta, Boston, Milwaukee, and Seattle—revealed "a perfect although indirect association [by rank] between the proportion of the population loss for the total community" . . . and the proportion and size of the population of color living therein (Willie 1984:199). These facts indicate that cultural implications of demographic trends in cities must be analyzed carefully before deriving cause-and-effect propositions. The tendency to attribute most of the change in racial composition of city populations to school desegregation is too simplistic.

The factors discussed above must be taken into account when observing that Boston's school population had changed from predominantly White in 1970, to predominantly people of color. Today, the largest student population in the Boston public schools is African American.

In the wake of the *Morgan* case, Blacks had begun to attain greater access to the centers of municipal power. Perhaps the strongest early indicator of this increased access was the 1977 election of John O'Bryant to Boston's five-member School Committee. O'Bryant became the first African American elected to this body in the twentieth century. As a member of a racial minority, O'Bryant led the effort to bring African American leadership to the superintendency. In 1978, O'Bryant's first year on the committee, Robert Wood, a former University of Massachusetts president, was appointed superintendent, becoming the first Boston public school superintendent not to have risen through the ranks of school bureaucracy. Wood helped to break the practice of insider and Irish leadership for the superintendency.

Wood, who lasted two years in the position, was replaced by an "insider" Paul Kennedy who, in 1981, died unexpectedly of a heart attack. This set the stage for Spillane's appointment. In 1981, four years after the first African American was elected to the School Committee, another African American, Jean McGuire, was elected. Thus, the five-person School Committee had two Black members, a radical departure from Boston politics a decade earlier.

The passage of a referendum expanding the committee to thirteen members resulted in greater representation on the School Committee. Nine were to be elected from voter districts whose boundaries would be identical to those for the City Council and four would be elected at large. The City Council also changed to election by single-members districts. Black candidates (i.e., O'Bryant and McGuire) eventually won School Committee seats under the exclusively at-large election system. This system, however, which required citywide voter support for election, made it extremely difficult because most minority candidates could not afford to run citywide campaigns. The first thirteen-member Boston School Committee took office in 1984, the year before Laval Wilson's selection.

In 1985, when Wilson was chosen, the president of the Boston School Committee was John Nucci. Nucci, only thirty years old at the time, was Italian American and had served as the Community Affairs

Coordinator for Boston's oldest and largest anti-poverty agency, Action for Boston Community Development (ABCD). His election emphasized the growing importance of the Italian ethnic community in Boston politics.

Politically, Nucci was located near the center of a School Committee spectrum, which, for the sake of convenience, may be divided into two predictable factions: liberal and conservative. Liberals were strongly in favor of minority access, educational innovation, and school reform. Conservatives, by contrast, were more bound to an inbred school administrative network and to traditional modes of instruction. There were exceptions within both factions, of course, and on given occasions, members would take uncharacteristic positions. Generally, however, this accurately depicts the central tendencies of the ideological groups represented on the 1985 Boston School Committee.

An analysis of this new thirteen-member board's voting record during its first year revealed a 7 to 6 conservative majority on most closely contested issues. Members like O'Bryant and McGuire were in the liberal camp, while others, such as committee Treasurer Daniel Burke and committee member Rita Walsh-Tomasini, voted consistently with the conservatives. It is important to note here that Nucci was close enough to the spectrum's political center to win the presidency by gaining support from both factions. He supported some of the social and educational changes proposed by the liberals. He also had higher political ambitions, as subsequent events would attest— (Nucci won an at-large seat on the City Council). A successful superintendency search could raise his political profile.

In any case, when Spillane opted to move on—he had tired, he said, of the expanded committee's interference and had also found the Fairfax offer "too lucrative" to refuse—Nucci opted for a national superintendency search. This decision provided an opportunity for the broadest range of outsiders to apply, including Laval Wilson. While the precedent for this procedure had been set in the search that yielded "Bud" Spillane, there was not unanimous School Committee support for it on this occasion.

Nevertheless, Nucci's decision prevailed. He named Shirley Owens-Hicks, an African American woman and vice-president of the School Committee, as chair of the search body. Thus, after deliberating with her and the School Committee's other officer, Treasurer Daniel

Burke, Nucci selected the other Search Committee members. The total membership reached twenty-four when five School Committee members opted to join the committee's officers on the search panel.

Despite this expansion, the basic composition and character of the Search Committee was unchanged. It remained a large, broadly based and decidedly liberal unit. Its membership included individuals of the highest local prestige, including Mayor Flynn himself.

Other members of special stature were Robert Corrigan, the chancellor of the University of Massachusetts; John Delaney, a vice-president of the Bank of Boston; John Lawson, state Commissioner of Education; and John Robinson, president of the Boston NAACP chapter. Additional key members were Ellen Guiney, director of the City-Wide Education Coalition (CWEC), the city's principal school oversight organization; David Cortiella, head of El Comite, the city's largest Latino parent group; Edward Doherty, president of the Boston Teacher's Union (BTU); and Glenola Mitchell, from the City-wide Parent Council (CPC).

Of the Search Committee's twenty-four members, seven were African American and two Latino. Joining them were a sufficient number of liberals and progressives (e.g., Guiney, Corrigan, Delaney, Lawson, and, in this instance, Mayor Flynn) to form a Search Committee majority that maximized the chances of minority candidates. This situation, of course, did not please the School Committee's conservative faction. Given the stature of so many Search Committee members and the fact that any School Committee member who wished to do so could join the Search Committee, there remained, however, virtually no School Committee criticism on this issue.

Consistent with its liberal orientation, the Search Committee's majority was committed to including minority candidates among the finalists. David Cortiella, a prominent member of that majority stated this goal bluntly: "One, we wanted to stop McDonough [the acting Superintendent] and, two, we wanted to send the School Committee at least two strong minority candidates (Edwards 1989:122).

Stopping McDonough at the search level was a priority for liberals because of the conservative majority that controlled the School Committee. If McDonough reached the finals, it was generally felt that he had enough votes on the School Committee to win the superintendency. A quiet, accessible, and mannerly man, McDonough had risen through the ranks of the bureaucracy and had worked in the school system for over thirty years.

As a deputy superintendent he had previously served as acting superintendent (after Kennedy's death) and was now serving in that role again. Despite his self-effacing and amiable demeanor, in this situation McDonough's background made him a symbol to liberals of a discredited school bureaucracy.

McDonough did, indeed, have strong support on the School Committee, particularly in Joseph Casper, a vocal and flamboyant committee conservative who was often at the center of its volatile interpersonal dynamics. One could speculate, in fact, that Casper's support hurt McDonough more than it helped him since it served to unify liberal efforts to defeat McDonough's candidacy. In the end his candidacy was defeated, but in the struggle to save it, a revealing subplot emerged involving the candidacy of Laval Wilson.

Jack Robinson, the NAACP's Boston president and a Search Committee member, was openly supportive of Laval Wilson's candidacy from the outset. Like himself, Wilson was African American and conservative. Being the only Black candidate of stature who possessed these attributes, Wilson was the ideal choice of the leader of a traditional civil rights organization like the NAACP. Robinson, therefore, decided to launch an early, vigorous campaign on Wilson's behalf.

Joseph Casper, like Robinson, was educationally conservative, and for that reason, Casper claimed he was also attracted to Wilson. Casper's first choice for superintendent, however, was Joseph McDonough. Given the Search Committee's liberal majority, Casper was afraid that McDonough would not be among those recommended to the School Committee. So he and Robinson, as they both later acknowledged, struck a deal. Robinson would vote for McDonough in the Search Committee's final vote (at each stage of Search Committee voting, members could vote for as many as three candidates) and Casper would vote for Wilson on the first ballot of the School Committee's vote *if* Wilson became one of the finalists.

The openness of Casper's and Robinson's advocacy, however, was uncharacteristic of the Search Committee's internal deliberations, where partisan lobbying was carefully avoided. Cortiella, for example, strongly desired a Latino superintendent, but did not lobby for one (Negroni) until after the Search Committee's work was done. "There was a sense of history being written," Cortiella said, "and lobbying in that situation did not seem proper" (Edwards 1989:117–18).

Nor did it require lobbying for the Search Committee's liberal majority to realize its goal, which was to ensure that progressive and minority candidates were presented as finalists to the School Committee. Through ideological bonding and by supporting each other at every stage of the search process, their wills prevailed. Thus, when the vote to select finalists was taken at its June 26 meeting, the Search Committee's choices were Laval Wilson, an African American; Peter Negroni, a Hispanic American; and Larry Cuban, a White liberal and educational progressive.

Because the June 26, 1985 vote had been taken by secret ballot and since McDonough had failed to make the final list, Casper and School Committee member John Grady initiated legal action to invalidate the vote. In a subsequent vote, however, taken by open ballot on July 12, the Search Committee selected the same three finalists.

After the June 26 ballot, when the names of the finalists became known, it did not take long for a campaign on behalf of Laval Wilson to begin, one that openly appealed to racial sentiment. On July 4, 1985, Boston's leading Black weekly, the *Bay State Banner*, ran a front page editorial that began: "Boston needs a Black Superintendent of Schools." The editorial went on to urge support for Wilson, stating that it was only "fair and appropriate that Boston now select a qualified Black leader of its schools." Erroneously claiming that "more than 60% of [Boston's] public school students are black" (the actual figure was 48%), the editors viewed Wilson as "an encouraging symbol" to head the Boston public schools at that time.

The editorial then proceeded to exert pressure on the School Committee's minority members. "In order for Wilson to be selected," the editors wrote, "he must garner the votes of seven School Committee members. A solid vote from John O'Bryant, Jean McGuire, Grace Romero and Shirley Owens-Hicks would provide four votes." The editorial was titled, "A Golden Opportunity."

Subsequent *Banner* editorials increased pressure on the School Committee's Blacks, particularly on O'Bryant and McGuire, who were thought to favor Negroni. Pressure on behalf of Wilson reached a point, in fact, where some felt that it threatened to divide the Black and Latino communities. To address this situation, a coalition of Black and Latino organizations held a press conference on July 24, at which it chastised certain Black leaders for attempting to "bully" Black School Committee members. The spokesperson for the group, James Jennings, of the Black Political Task Force, accused Robinson and Melvin Miller, the *Banner*'s editor and publisher, of sacrificing "the needs of children to petty ethnocentric considerations," and of supporting Wilson "for no other reason than skin pigmentation." Robinson and Miller denied these charges. Other organizations represented at the conference were the Rainbow Coalition, Blacks for Empowerment, the Latino Political Action Committee, and El Comite.

Negroni's supporters had made efforts on his behalf, but less openly and in a less confrontational manner than had the supporters of Wilson. And Cortiella was very much at the forefront of those efforts.

"I simply lobbied all of the School Committee members," he said. "That's what lobbying is, you go see the people and make your case. They got used to seeing me on the eleventh floor [the School Committee's offices at 26 Court Street]. I told them to put blinders on, to forget about skin color. Negroni was simply the best man to lead the system after Spillane had restored its respectability. I told them that they needed a progressive educator at this point, someone to take the system in a modern direction. I tried to stick to educational philosophy and stay away from the race issue" (Edwards 1989:134).

Among the members of the School Committee to whom Cortiella spoke was Grace Romero. Romero was the School Committee's only Latino member but she did not come out in favor of Negroni. Moreover, her cryptic, unpredictable style made Cortiella wary of her. "But I had to speak to her," Cortiella said, "she was on the Committee. I knew she was unpredictable, but I had to do it" (Edwards 1989:134).

Romero, as events would unfold, encountered serious legal difficulties during the period of the search. These troubles were caused mainly by signatures that had been gathered on her petition for renomination to serve on the School Committee. A July 17 article in the *Boston Herald* quoted Election Commission Chairman Michael Joyce as saying that his office had found "what appears to be fraudulent signatures" on Romero's petitions. The article pictured a portion of one petition on which the same names appeared more than once but in "dramatically different handwriting" (Edwards 1989:135).

Romero was indicted in August on charges of filing campaign papers with false signatures. Later, she charged that Cortiella, acting for the mayor, had attempted to bribe her with an offer of $10,000 to vote for Negroni. All parties denied Romero's allegations. A spokesperson for Flynn characterized them as "the height of ridiculousness" (Edwards 1989:135). Cortiella called them "outright lies."

Romero, in any case, did not vote for Negroni, in spite of pressure from segments of the Latino community. "I voted for Wilson because I honestly believed he was the best candidate," she said. "I checked him out with people in Rochester, people such as parents and administrators who ought to know. And I got good reports. He was simply the best candidate" (Edwards 1989:135).

Robinson confirmed that Romero had told him she would vote for Wilson. "Hers was the most courageous vote of all, Black or White," Robinson said. "She was the only Hispanic on the School Committee and was under tremendous pressure, but she took a stand and stuck by it" (Edwards 1989:136).

Cortiella's failure to gain Romero's support did not discourage him, however, since he had not really expected it. He regarded her as only one of thirteen members he needed to attempt to persuade. Other Latino organizations, such as Alianza Hispana and the Hispanic Office of Planning and Evaluation (HOPE) informed Romero of their support for Negroni, but she refused to budge.

The open lobbying now under way for Wilson and Negroni signaled a shift in the search's focus to the School Committee itself. No similar efforts were made on behalf of Cuban. The School Committee had meaningful options to choose from among the candidates presented to it.

CANDIDATE PROFILES

Laval Wilson was forty-nine, African American, and the superintendent of the Rochester, New York, public schools, a system of approximately 34,000 students. Wilson earned his doctorate from Northwestern University and had previously held superintendencies in Berkeley, California (for six years), and in a city on Long Island, New York (for one year). He had also previously served as an assistant superintendent, a principal, and a teacher.

Wilson had a reputation as a stern, no-nonsense administrator, one who was a hard worker and who drove his staff hard as well. He had been raised on Chicago's South Side, and was, therefore, no stranger to the realities of inner-city life. Joseph Hill, a former superintendent of schools under whom Wilson served as an assistant superintendent and principal in Evanston, Illinois, during the late 1960s, described Wilson as "a bulldog. If it can be done," Hill said, "Laval Wilson can do it. He wouldn't take 'no' for an answer" (*Boston Globe*, Aug. 2, 1985).

Peter Negroni also knew the inner city firsthand, having learned it on the streets of New York City where he grew up and from his immersion in the politics of the Latino school district in the Bronx, where he had been a superintendent since 1978. Negroni, forty-three years old, was of Puerto Rican descent and held a doctorate from Fairleigh Dickinson University. New York City's school system of approximately one million students is divided into thirty-two districts, each with a nine-member school board. These districts administer elementary and middle schools, while the seven-member central Board of Education operates the high schools and sets overall policy for the system. Local boards hire superintendents and principals, and control the districts' budgets. Negroni's district (District 12) had approximately 18,000 students, which made it a fairly large district in the system.

Negroni had served twenty-two years in the New York City school system, most of that time in the Bronx, where he had been a principal for seven years, prior to becoming a superintendent in 1978. He was a pioneer in implementing bilingual education programs and was known for his political skills.

Larry Cuban, age fifty, was both the only White educator among the finalists and the only practicing academic. Cuban had been an associate professor of education at Stanford University since 1981. He earned his doctorate at Stanford and published articles and books about urban education. Prior to coming to Stanford, Cuban had served as a superintendent of schools in Arlington, Virginia, a district of 20,000 students. His educational experience totaled thirty years. From his writings and previous superintendency one could regard Cuban as an educational progressive.

These differences among the candidates were well illustrated by certain responses from the candidates during their July 19 interviews before the School Committee. Laval Wilson, interviewed last, was clearly the most conservative of the three and also the most self-assertive, claiming, for example, that he was "the most qualified urban educator in the United States" (Edwards 1989:144).

Wilson also made it a point during the interviews to discount the racial significance of his candidacy. That point of view troubled some African Americans, including O'Bryant who, nevertheless, would strongly support him later on. Wilson's educational conservatism was well captured during the interviews by the following response, which he hoped would illustrate the soundness of his strict remedial approach:

My wife and I have four youngsters that all play musical instruments. The music teacher always knows which youngster didn't practice during the week. If the kids practice all week and take the music lessons on Saturday, then they are doing pretty well.

That concept can be expanded to education. Practice, practice, practice. I know a very few things that more practice doesn't help. So if youngsters practice more writing, more reading skills, under the supervision of a skilled professional—and arithmetic—those skill levels will go up. (Edwards 1989:146)

Cuban, by contrast, placed his remedial focus on the professional development of teachers:

But, obviously, remediation has to begin in the regular classroom with the teacher and the first bunch of kids that they get early on.

Teachers need to have the support and the expanded repertoire of skills needed to deal with a wide range of abilities and achievement within their classroom. That is where the heart of remediation begins.

What I am talking about is extensive staff development of teachers and principals. That is what I would call the fundamental issue. (Edwards 1989:146–147)

Peter Negroni's pedagogical position seemed to be located somewhere between those of Cuban and Wilson. With the exception of bilingual education, which was his specialty, his orientation was more that of a generalist's than theirs. Negroni's strength, as he saw it, was his ability to work cooperatively with broad constituencies. This became a theme to which he persistently referred during his interview. Speaking of the conflicts that he experienced with his own school board and his ability to survive those conflicts, Negroni said:

The asset that I have is that I have done it; I have been in trouble with the board and I have learned how to work with the board and bring them together, so I have the experience of bringing a board together.

I also have a good sense of working with people, and I can't say anything about the other candidates, if they have that sense, but I know that I am very, very able and capable when it comes to working with people and resolving issues with people.

I am a "cohesor." I bring people together. I don't push them apart and I think, as evidenced by everything that I have seen during the last month and a half, we very much need that in Boston. (Edwards 1989:148)

Here, then, were clearly discernible different educational options to choose from despite the intensely political nature of the selection process. Indeed, it was only when the political aims of key actors in that process conflicted with their educational preferences that dilemmas arose for them.

Those who either felt no such dilemmas or resolved them early were free to seize the political initiative. This is why both Robinson and Cortiella were able to launch early, sustained campaigns on behalf of their chosen candidates. This is why Casper was quickly able to embrace Wilson as a second choice once McDonough had fallen, and why O'Bryant's support for Wilson was so late in emerging.

O'Bryant initially did not identify with Wilson because he doubted the strength of Wilson's commitment to Black interests. This doubt was only strengthened, O'Bryant felt, by the site visits he made to Wilson's former school districts. Returning from a conference in Oregon, which he attended during the search period, O'Bryant stopped off at Berkeley, then traveled east to Rochester, New York. Like the other School Committee members who visited Wilson's former districts, O'Bryant, too, was impressed by Wilson's professional successes and by the esteem in which he was held by civic, educational, and business elements in those cities. O'Bryant was also disturbed by Wilson's relations with the cities' Black communities. Asked specifically about this, he responded:

Well, it was the same problem everywhere. Trouble with Black folk. In Berkeley, it had to do with Black teachers and seniority. When there was a conflict with the union over layoffs (I think it was around 1975), he wasn't really with us. In Rochester, the anti-poverty people were concerned that he didn't relate. It's a problem, man. (Edwards 1989:164)

But in the end, O'Bryant felt he had no choice except to support Wilson. "I took a gamble," he said. "I felt that I had to. We would just have to find a way to work with him, to try to straighten his head out" (Edwards 1989:165).

By this time, however, Wilson had already gained the support of Robinson and Casper. Yet O'Bryant was determined to ensure Wilson's victory himself. He did not trust the committee's conservatives in racial matters (which he saw this case to be), and he had always led the committee on such matters himself. It was O'Bryant's belated decision to campaign for Wilson that provided the search's final drama, which can be reduced to three basic subplots. One was the open campaign on Wilson's behalf headed by Casper and Robinson; second, the more quiet effort led by Cortiella in behalf of Negroni; and third, O'Bryant's own belated campaign to direct and gain credit for a Wilson victory.

The separate campaigns of Casper and O'Bryant, in fact, produced an amusing final irony on the School Committee. Casper and the committee's conservatives soon became angry with O'Bryant for actually *agreeing* with them. Both wanted a Wilson superintendency, but since the conservatives felt they already had the votes to accomplish this result, they preferred that O'Bryant, a long-standing political enemy, oppose them.

O'Bryant, on the other hand, was unsuccessful in convincing several members of his own liberal bloc to vote for Wilson. Therefore, while the conservatives might have gained a Wilson victory without O'Bryant's support, which seems doubtful, O'Bryant certainly could not have achieved such a victory without them.

In the case of O'Bryant's liberal colleagues, all of whom favored a minority superintendent, several just could not bring themselves to vote for an educational conservative like Wilson. Jean McGuire, who was Black, voted for Negroni. So did other traditional O'Bryant allies, such as Abigail Browne, William Marchionne, and Kevin McCluskey. The committee's Blacks, with the exception of McGuire, voted for Wilson and were joined by the conservative majority to give Wilson a 9 to 4 victory. Cuban did not receive any votes, which suggests a unanimous minority mandate in this particular search.

Where Negroni's campaign was concerned, Cortiella and others had, indeed, hoped for O'Bryant's vote. They had counted on it, in fact, until the eleventh hour, when it became evident that O'Bryant would vote for Wilson (Edwards 1989: 161). Had they received O'Bryant's vote, at least Nucci would have been prepared to vote for Negroni and Walsh-Tomasini might have abstained.

As committee president, Nucci voted last. He cast his ballot for Wilson, he said, because at this point, Wilson had already won. "When I went downstairs [from his office to the auditorium on July 31] I was prepared to. . . vote for Negroni," Nucci said. "He was more progressive than Wilson. . . but by the time my turn came, Wilson had it won, so I [simply] provided a better margin" (Edwards 1989:160).

For her part, Walsh-Tomasini considered not voting at all because "I was [still] for McDonough." Tomasini only voted for Wilson, she said, "because he was the better of two evils, you might say" (Edwards 1989:160).

Negroni hypothetically, might have gained six votes, with Walsh-Tomasini abstaining. This would have denied a majority to either candidate and required a second ballot, in which case, Negroni might have won. In fact, then, O'Bryant was instrumental in Wilson's victory, not because he persuaded others to vote for Wilson, but because he himself voted for Wilson instead of for Negroni. One realizes from this analysis that Wilson's 9 to 4 victory was not at all the mandate it appeared to be.

TENURE AND DISMISSAL

Nevertheless, Laval Wilson's appointment was significant. He became the first African American to head the nation's oldest public school system and the second successive outsider to do so. If, in fact, he had not acquired the mandate from the School Committee that he appeared to, Wilson still received strong early support from a city that was trying to repair its tarnished racial image and recapture control of its schools from the Federal Court.

It is useful, however, to look beyond the initial rush of goodwill toward Wilson and note at least two important factors that would prove critical to his tenure: the reform orientation of Boston's business community, and Wilson's formal, bureaucratic, and essentially raceless persona.

Wilson arrived in Boston with the reputation of having worked well with business communities during his former superintendencies. Clearly, the image he projected as a no-nonsense, efficient manager resonated well in business environments where similar styles are often found. However, Boston's business leadership, in 1985, was also responsive to a national school reform movement, which, by then, had gathered strong momentum. This reform orientation was manifest in the evolution of the Boston Compact.

The Boston Compact is an agreement between Boston's public schools and many of the city's business organizations. In it, the schools agree to meet specified performance goals in exchange for higher educational and job opportunities that businesses would provide for students. First signed in 1982, the compact soon became a model for similar arrangements in other urban cities. As Daniel F. Morley, vice-president of Boston's State Street Bank and former president of the city's Private Industry Council (PIC), stated shortly after the first compact was signed:

The business community began to see that its self-interests would be served if the problems of school-to-work transition were given more emphasis in public education. At the same time, we recognized that we could and should insist that if we were to provide greater numbers of jobs, the School Department needed to assume greater responsibility for curriculum improvement, instructional quality and the retention of students. . . . So, we began planning for the Compact. (Edwards 1989:72–73)

Student performance measures were of the traditional variety, centering mainly on student achievement in reading and mathematics. However, from the compact's inception student goals were not being satisfactorily met. Moreover, over the years the business community became increasingly impatient with both the performance of the School Department and the behavior of the Boston School Committee, which often seemed more concerned with internal rivalries than with setting effective school policies. Eventually, the business community concluded that the School Committee structure needed to be changed, and it supported a protracted but eventually successful effort to accomplish this result.

Given the reformist attitude of Boston's business community, along with its growing dissatisfaction with the school system's governing mechanism, one had to wonder about its long-term relationships with a superintendent who had a traditional orientation toward education that some might call conservative.

Where race was concerned, one notes how consistently Wilson stressed its irrelevance to the technical performance of his duties. The essence of this position was captured during the search process in a statement he made to the School Committee's interviewing panel on July 19, 1985:

A Superintendent, whether that person is black or white or Hispanic or Asian or some other group, makes some very similar decisions on budgets, curricula determination, all the various issues that come before the superintendent every day. I happen to be Black, my profession is school educator and school superintendent. I would hope that the entire community and the School Committee would support me as a candidate. (Edwards 1989:144–45)

Boston, however, had a recent history of intense racial conflict. Moreover, as its first African American superintendent, Wilson would represent an undeniable symbol of the increased access that Boston's Blacks had been fighting so long to attain. Technically, then, race might not have mattered to Wilson's superintendency, but politically, socially, and historically his superintendency mattered very much to Boston's racial evolution. As an African American, Wilson could only ignore this fact at his own peril. Indeed, Wilson himself conceded that he might have been more attentive to cultivating support within the African American community. In a city that had a reputation for racial animus, Wilson said he wanted "to downplay the fact that the city might have appointed a superintendent just because he was Black. I was trying to at least let everybody know that a Black person could relate to everybody, could be fair to all. . . . I didn't take strong Black positions because I had a broad mixture of kids" (Wilson interview, April 19, 1996).

On the other hand, Wilson acknowledged that "it probably would have been better to have spent more time working with certain Black leaders like Mel [King], Hubie [Jones], and [James] Jennings. I got caught up in so many other things. . . . but I probably should have tried to [create] a better bridge." In any event, the absence of strong Black support at the demise of Wilson's superintendency contrasted sharply with its prominence during the campaign to appoint him. In both cases, the level of Black support made a difference.

Against this background, Wilson launched a superintendency that can be conveniently divided into two parts: first, the early or "honeymoon," phase, which lasted perhaps until early 1988; then the final, conflict-ridden phase, which ended with the School Committee's buying out his contract in 1990.

The centerpiece of Wilson's "honeymoon" period was his Boston Education Plan, a blueprint for school improvement that required over two years to develop. Indeed, the process through which this plan was created consumed most of his honeymoon period. This is the period when new leaders may be permitted to implement radical programs. Wilson, however, opted to be more gradual than radical, more comprehensive than quick. "If we could take the broad view," he said, "I felt that we could intelligently address all the main problems. . . and, with time, that's what I tried to do" (Wilson interview, April 19, 1996).

Wilson's strategy for developing this plan called for the creation of sixteen task forces, each charged with examining a separate educational issue. The issues were identified through mailed surveys to education stakeholders inside and outside the school system. The returned results were tabulated to identify major areas of concern, and the task forces that examined them were asked to submit recommendations to the superintendent. Altogether, there were approximately 350 task force members, representing a broad cross section of the Boston community (Beaumont 1993:158). The sixteen areas or issues were: adolescent issues; at-risk students; counseling and guidance; curriculum support; early childhood programs and early intervention; facilities; instructional materials; mathematics; middle and high school programs; parent and community support; professional development of teachers and school administrators; reading; safe and orderly school environments; special education, bilingual and vocational/occupational/career education, student assignment process and quality desegregated education; and writing (Beaumont 1993:157).

After receiving task force reports and discussing them with his cabinet, Wilson decided which recommendations he would incorporate into the plan and present to the School Committee for approval. The plan itself was an exceedingly bulky document that was submitted to School Committee members only three days before the June 22, 1987, meeting at which it was to be considered. The committee required another meeting to complete its deliberations, and reconvened on July 1, at which time the plan was quickly approved.

The relatively rapid approval of such a voluminous and critically important document illustrated, at once, the Boston School Committee's disinclination to dwell upon educational matters and the process through which superintendents can sometimes become de facto policymakers. When two committee members, Abigail Browne and Juanita Wade, requested public hearings for the plan because of its far-reaching importance, they were voted down. In effect, the plan quickly became a referendum on Wilson himself. Members of the committee who supported Wilson, and they were a clear majority at this point, discouraged extended debate on the matter fearing it might imply lack of support for the superintendent. This attitude was expressed succinctly during the proceedings by committee President Nucci who, despite early reservations, had become part of Wilson's School Committee majority: "He [Dr. Wilson] has brought his 30 years experience as a professional educator and put it on the table in front of us." Nucci said, "That's good enough for me" (Beaumont 1993:158). Thus, the superintendent, rather than the content of his proposal, became the central issue. Wilson's document was easily passed. His public support was still strong.

It was now 1987, however, and the honeymoon period of his candidacy would soon end. Wilson, in effect, had bought time through his planning process. Final judgments about how well he was addressing substantive school issues had been implicitly postponed. Only now, in fact, with the passage of his plan, had specific issues and concrete strategies for addressing them been formulated.

Wilson had thus created for himself the time and space to consolidate his superintendency without being held strictly accountable for the system's worst deficiencies. In some respects, he had used this period well. For example, he had either instituted or laid the groundwork for certain administrative changes that were quite important.

Among these decisions was reflected a firm if quiet commitment on his part for affirmative action: Wilson appointed the first Blacks to hold the positions of Facilities Director, Food Service Director, and Police Chief of School Safety. He also appointed the first Asian and first Latino individuals to positions of zone superintendent. In addition, in conjunction with Boston University in 1986, Wilson co-developed a training institute for the system's administrators. In 1985, he created Project Promise at the Timilty Middle School. Project Promise was a pilot instructional program whose success at Timilty, one of the city's poorest performing schools, later earned the school an achievement award from the president of the United States. These were important, but relatively unnoticed, accomplishments that could be traced to the earliest stages of Wilson's superintendency. It is ironic and significant, however, that just when his blueprint for substantial educational changes had been ratified, Wilson's support on the School Committee and elsewhere began to erode.

An early signal of this erosion was a credit card issue that arose in December 1987. Wilson requested and had been granted a corporate credit card by the School Committee, although no other city official, including the mayor, owned one. "The chief executive officer of most companies, along with their vice presidents normally have corporate cards," Wilson was quoted as having said in a *Boston Herald* article (December 18, 1987). According to the same news story, Wilson allegedly misused the card by taking unauthorized cash advances and accruing high finance charges by failing to promptly submit receipts.

Wilson denied the charges, demanded a front page retraction from the *Herald*, and hinted at a lawsuit, calling the story "misleading" and "approaching libel" (*BPS in Brief*, CWEC, December 1987). Neither the retraction nor the lawsuit materialized, however, although the allegations against Wilson were never publicly verified by the city comptroller's office. The incident, however, caused problems for School Committee treasurer Dan Burke.

Because he was treasurer, Burke was held responsible by committee colleagues for allowing the alleged card irregularity to occur. Burke, in turn, became quite disenchanted with Wilson, although he had been Wilson's earliest supporter on the School Committee, earlier, even, than Casper or O'Bryant. Another source of tension between Burke and Wilson at the time was Wilson's refusal to allow Jim Walsh, his deputy superintendent, to supervise an internship Burke needed for the doctoral program in which he had enrolled. Wilson saw this decision as avoiding a conflict of interest (Wilson interview, April 19, 1996).

In any event, the loss of Burke's support marked the beginning of Wilson's loss of support among the School Committee's conservative majority. Without it, several of Wilson's educational positions became vulnerable. Among those positions were a "deficit model" approach to underachieving students; strict promotional policies that increased student holdover rates, particularly in the early grades; and a reluctance to embrace school-based management. Indeed, one of Wilson's first acts as superintendent was to cut the school-based management office's budget by $235,000. These unpopular recommendations seriously damaged his image among important stakeholders in the school community (Beaumont 1993:165).

Some African American professionals, such as Hubie Jones, former dean of Boston University's School of Social Work, interim president of Roxbury Community College, and a member of Mayor Flynn's School Reform Task Force, publicly withdrew support of Wilson. Jones was also head of the Human Services Collaborative, a consortium of health and social service agencies that served predominantly minority communities.

Wilson also did not support the collaborative's proposal to install health clinics in Boston's high schools (Beaumont 1993:163). This was one of the decisions Wilson, in retrospect, said he regretted most. In an interview in 1996, Wilson stated:

It was a tactical error on my part. I tried to walk on water . . . and things didn't quite come out right. We [he and Jones] had reached an agreement that I would support the pilot concept.

However, if I insisted upon clinics for all the high schools, then the pilot might have been a compromise. But my basis was that it would have been too costly. I had to close schools, and it didn't make good economic sense to me to have 19 high schools and a clinic in each. . . .

I had Hubie's support, I felt, up until that time. Politically, I should have gotten the pilot through. The *Boston Globe* supported it [and] . . . there probably would have been enough votes. In retrospect, I might have tried for two reasons; it might have been a good idea to see how a pilot would have worked and, secondly, I lost some people who might have been supportive of the schools. . . .

The decision-making process lost support. I used up capital for other efforts, like the single basal reader, for example. It got through, but a situation had now been set up that was either for or against Wilson. (Wilson interview, 1996)

The time had also arrived when Wilson was headed for trouble with Boston's business community. Aside from being perceived as resisting school-based management, a reform the business community strongly endorsed, Wilson had not succeeded in raising student achievement to the levels agreed upon in the Boston Compact. With the compact's 1989 renewal date approaching, Boston's business leadership had begun to express strong dissatisfaction with the performance of students in the public schools (Beaumont 1993:165).

Wilson had a plan in place, but hard facts regarding student achievement were bound to surface on the occasion of compact renewal. The results confirmed that Boston's students were not achieving satisfactorily. The achievement of seniors was of special interest in this instance since seniors would go on to higher education or enter the job market. Academically, Boston's seniors in fact were not doing well. For example, the Citywide Educational Coalition (CWEC) reported that in 1987 the median SAT scores for Boston's seniors were 150 points lower than for seniors nationwide. In 1988, their scores were a little higher but still ranked below Massachusetts's and the national averages. Worse, in 1988, 24 percent of Boston's seniors scored below 240 in verbal skills, a score that translates to a ratio of approximately 9 correct responses in 85 (*BPS in Brief*, August 1988). These facts combined with the overall underachievement of Boston's students represented a serious concern.

Therefore, in 1989, when Wilson's own contract was up for renewal, it came as no surprise that he barely gained an extension. Indeed, circumstances in 1989, both for Wilson's superintendency and for the Boston School Committee, were distinctly unfavorable. As our next case study will show, a concerted effort led by the mayor and Boston's business community was then under way to replace the elected School Committee with a mayorally appointed board.

Since its inception, the thirteen–member School Committee had openly discredited itself through a series of conspicuous policy failures. These included: a general failure to attend to policy issues despite special legislation in 1988 (Chapter 613) that relieved it of time-consuming personnel responsibilities; failure to develop a new student-assignment plan in a timely fashion after a Federal Appeals Court, in 1987, indicated that more flexible racial guidelines for student assignments in the school desegregation case were now permissible; and failure, almost every year, to balance its annual budget.

Wilson, of course, was a party to some of the committee's failures and was increasingly viewed by School Committee critics as part of the problem. It was Wilson, for example, who counseled the School Committee against changing the student assignment plan he had earlier recommended in his Boston Education Plan. He would not propose a way to develop an alternative student assignment plan, although the Appeals Court's decision provided an opportunity to do so. The mayor, in effect, usurped the superintendent's role by retaining consultants to develop a plan, since Wilson and the School Committee had failed to act with dispatch. Although it was still not satisfied with Dr. Wilson's leadership, the business community did renew the Boston Compact in 1988. The business community also helped the School Committee negotiate a teacher's contract that mandated school-based management. Despite Wilson's involvement in these matters, they appeared to be the result of the business community's initiatives rather than the superintendent's leadership.

On the School Committee, where members were elected every two years, a shift had taken place in voting alignments. Wilson still held a narrow 7 to 6 majority but it had become more tenuous than ever. Shirley Owens-Hicks had left the committee to run for and win a seat in the state legislature. She was replaced by Gerald Anderson, also an African American, who continued to support Wilson. However, Anderson was not as well connected in the community as Owens-Hicks. In the wake of her legal problems, Grace Romero lost to Juanita Wade in the election that fall. Wade, who was African American, continued to support Wilson as Romero had.

Indeed, Wilson's support had become increasingly based upon racial considerations. Jean McGuire, for example, shifted her support to Wilson although she voted for another candidate during the search process. She believed that much of the opposition to Wilson on the School Committee was racist. Thus, in 1989, with most of his conservative support gone, Wilson's contract was renewed through the united vote of the committee's four black members (O'Bryant, McGuire, Wade, and Anderson) and by John Grady, the one White conservative who stuck by him to the end. The moderates, John Nucci and Thomas O'Reilly, also continued to support Wilson.

Casper was no longer on the School Committee (he had run unsuccessfully for a City Council seat), and both Burke and Walsh-Tomasini had withdrawn their support of Wilson. Others on the committee in 1989 were Abigail Browne, Robert Cappucci, Kitty Bowman, and Peggy Davis-Mullen, all of whom opposed renewal of Wilson's contract.

The renewal itself was anything but a strong endorsement of Wilson's leadership. It was a two-year contract divided into one-year segments that required a performance evaluation every six months. After each evaluation, the contract could be terminated by a majority vote of the School Committee. The contract also excluded two of Wilson's main requests: a 5 percent increase in his $95,000 annual salary, and an $18,000 housing allowance (Beaumont 1993:108). In addition, the contract contained a clause entitling Wilson to salary payments for the remainder of any buyout year, along with the monetary value of his accrued vacation days, in the event his contract was terminated.

Inclusion in the contract of buyout options did not set well for Wilson's future. Nor did committee member Cappucci's statement after the vote that "six members felt the contract should not be renewed. . . . We will do everything in our power to get a new superintendent" (Beaumont 1993:168).

In the past, Wilson's evaluations by the School Committee had been, more or less, pro forma. Both of them, one in 1986, the other in 1987, were conducted quietly, utilizing a National School Board Association rating form. On both occasions, Wilson was rated "superior," although the 1987 evaluation was delayed. The delay was caused by Wilson's job searches for new positions outside Boston, which included an application for the chancellorship of the New York City school system. This action, along with Wilson's 1988 request for an early indication from the committee regarding his 1989 renewal prospects, created doubts about Wilson's own long-term employment agenda.

In any case, the superintendent's evaluation had never seemed to be an urgent School Committee matter in the past. Past evaluations had not been based on pre-established goals, as was now the case. In fact, the School Committee was not in the habit of setting specific education goals. Instead, it had relied upon the superintendent to do so, as Wilson had done through his Boston Education Plan.

In this case, goals were being set, not so much to guide the system as to justify actions against the superintendent. But as *Boston Globe* columnist Alan Lupo wrote at the time: The "School Committee [was] foolish to set goals for Wilson to meet, because most of the members certainly knew the odds against Wilson remaining even if he met the goals. He alienated too many people, both consumers and potential allies of the system, and they include Blacks, Hispanics and Asians" (in Beaumont 1993:171), or as African American *Globe* columnist Robert Jordan agreed: "It's not only Wilson's performance that has gotten him into. . . difficulty. It is his personality. . . the abrasiveness that has turned off even those School Committee members who agree with most of his stances" (in Beaumont 1993:172).

Wilson, in fact, met most of the School Committee's goals because, with the assistance of an evaluation subcommittee headed by O'Bryant, he was allowed to select goals himself. The whole process, however, only seemed to postpone the inevitable.

The inevitable—specifically Wilson's firing—was ensured when both Nucci and O'Reilly decided not to run for re-election in 1989. Nucci, instead, ran for an at-large City Council seat and won; O'Reilly simply withdrew from educational politics. Predictably, their replacements, Stephen Holt and Marianne Elo, had run on a platform that faulted the school system's leadership. Wilson, consequently, lost the narrow majority that Nucci and O'Reilly had provided.

Given the fact that Daniel Burke, now a staunch Wilson opponent, was elected president of the 1990 School Committee, Wilson's buyout became a virtual certainty. Burke also managed to add a second page to Wilson's evaluation form relating to community relations, and Wilson's ratings in this area were unsatisfactory.

At the School Committee's February 13, 1990, public meeting, Burke himself made the motion to buy out Wilson's contract and it was seconded by Stephen Holt. Burke then called for a discussion of buyout terms, whereupon the four Black members and Wilson's lone White ally, John Grady, walked out of the meeting. Of the remaining eight members, seven voted to buy out the contract; only one, Marianne Elo, opposed the motion. Laval Wilson's superintendency had ended.

WHEN RACE DOES AND DOES NOT MATTER: AN ANALYSIS OF THE ORDEAL OF BOSTON'S FIRST BLACK SUPERINTENDENT

On July 31, 1985, Laval Wilson, an African American educator, was named superintendent of the Boston public schools. This was a radical action for a school system that had been struggling with the issue of school desegregation and racial equity for more than two centuries. Ralph Smith, a professor of law who traced the complex events of school desegregation litigation in Boston, said that U.S. District Court Judge W. Arthur Garrity, Jr.'s order, which cited the Boston School Committee for intentionally carrying out a systematic program of segregation affecting all of the city's students, teachers, and school facilities, "set in motion a chain of events that . . . would permanently affect the city of Boston" (Smith 1978: 26). It is fair to characterize the selection of an African American to lead the Boston school system as an indirect outcome of Judge Garrity's court order, although the appointment did not happen until a decade later and was not a requirement of the remedy.

Up to the time of the 1974 decision of the *Morgan vs. Hennigan* case, Boston policymakers in government and public education were largely Irish in ancestry (Smith 1978:30). During the school desegregation crisis of the mid-1970s and before, "primary responsibility for the public school system in the city of Boston [was] vested in the Boston school Committee, a five-member body elected at large by the voters for four-year terms" (Smith 1978:32–33). In the decade preceding Judge Garrity's court order, only one person elected to the School Committee was not of Irish ancestry. Based on evidence presented in this case study, one may conclude that the educational establishment in Boston before court-ordered school desegregation was dominated by the Irish.

In an earlier century, Yankees of White Anglo Saxon Protestant background had controlled Boston politics. With the dramatically increasing Irish population in 1847, when over 37,000 Irish immigrants came to Boston, which then had a total population of approximately 114,000, the stage was set for an eventual challenge to Yankee political control and leadership. By 1920, it was clear that the Yankees had lost control of the city. They, therefore, retreated to the suburbs while the Irish consolidated their power over Boston (Smith 1978:29–30).

Similarly, the growing population of color should have been a signal that Irish power sooner or later would diminish. The number of people in a population's group is an important power resource. The year in which Judge Garrity issued his court order to desegregate the public schools, 35,024 people of color represented 39 percent of the school system's student body (Smith 1978:33). By 1985 when Wilson was appointed superintendent of schools, a majority of the students attending Boston's public schools were people of color, although they represented less than a majority of the city's total population.

In view of Boston's history of serial tribal control of the political establishment of the city and because numbers are a significant power resource, the trend toward an enlarged population of color caused this group to believe that its turn had come to provide leadership in education.

Wilson's contention that his race should not be one of the reasons for hiring him but that he should be retained simply because he is "the most qualified urban educator in the United States" seemed unrealistic, given the history of Boston, where racial and ethnic background have frequently been used as power resources.

Wilson's attitude could have resulted from the fact that several business leaders found him to be an attractive candidate because he had worked well with business communities in his previous superintendencies. Since business leadership has been a staple in local community power structures, Wilson may have calculated that his business support would provide him the power base he needed to implement his program, and that he would not be forced to play a people of color power card.

Wilson's attitude of downplaying his experience as the first Black superintendent in Boston also may have resulted from his having had this experience in other communities, like Berkeley and Rochester. It was neither new nor novel for him. What Wilson probably did not realize is that being the first Black superintendent was a big deal for Boston, although it was not a big deal for him, personally. The lesson to be learned from this is that communities may have needs that are different from those of some of their leaders. Leaders should not assume that their personal needs and those of the community are always the same.

We found no evidence that this was Wilson's thinking or strategy. However, his failure from the beginning to understand race as a power resource represented a fundamental misunderstanding of community organization, especially community power relations and decision making.

Robert Dahl's assertion that "the existence of multiple centers of power, none of which is wholly sovereign, will help to tame power . . . and settle conflicts peacefully" (Dahl 1967:24) should be taken seriously. An understanding of this reality could protect one who must direct and harmonize competing community interest groups, as a superintendent of schools necessarily must do, from committing the error of putting all of one's eggs in one basket.

It would appear that Wilson began his term as Boston's chief school officer relying too heavily on the business sector, only one of several community power centers. It should go without saying that one who attempts to fulfill the responsibilities of a school superintendent by relying too heavily on race or ethnicity as a single power resource is also likely to be stalled in program implementation. The principle is that local communities in the United States consist of several centers of power, some of which are more useful and others less useful for the implementation of particular educational programs. Moreover, it is essential to recognize that all power centers, including those that exist among racial and ethnic subdominant people of power, possess veto capacity. Thus, to ally oneself to some degree with a single power center like business is fatal for school superintendents and public officials who aspire to be effective community leaders.

While Wilson, in effect, was distancing himself from his racial minority constituency as a way of making himself more attractive to all of the people, most of the people of color on the Search Committee embraced him and worked furiously to ensure his election. The slate of finalists presented to the School Committee consisted of people who had worked outside Boston and who were not Irish. This slate was different from the one usually presented when the services of a new superintendent were needed. This was a consequence, in part, because of the desire of the School Committee chair to conduct a nationwide search and, in part, because of the presence of racial and ethnic minority members on the Search Committee. These two realities were innovations in the way that Boston's political and educational policymakers selected a new education leader.

These innovations were introduced not so much because of a change of attitude by the prevailing population. (The violent resistance to school desegregation is evidence of ongoing prejudice among many Bostonians.) Rather, as stated before, they were a consequence of changes in the kinds of people who served on the School Committee as decision makers.

Election by individual districts as well as at-large replaced the old method of citywide, at-large elections that tended to favor an Irish sweep exclusively and usually resulted in school committee victories for Whites only. From the new combination method of district and citywide elections, four people of color were added to the School Committee and a person of Italian ancestry was elected chair. Thus, changes in the kinds of people who served on the Boston School Committee and in their characteristics and experiences contributed to changes in the way the committee did its business.

These outcomes confirm an observation set forth by Leonard Duhl, a community psychiatrist and former federal public administrator. At the Harvard Seminar on Planning and Evaluation sponsored by the Laboratory of Community Psychiatry in the Medical College, Duhl said that the quickest way to change an organization is to change its clients (quoted in Willie 1978:91). This wise statement recognizes the fact that groups and individuals are interrelated, that groups depend on individuals for their effectiveness, and that individuals depend on groups for their effectiveness.

Consequently, when the membership of a group changes, there tends to be changes in its practices and policies. This is precisely what happened with the Boston School Committee. The chair, John Nucci when Wilson was invited to Boston, was affiliated with an ethnic group other than the Irish group that had prevailed for decades. Nucci decided it was time to open up the search process for a new superintendent. However, the people of color appointed to the Search Committee were so few that they could not meet the minimum critical mass of at least one-fifth that enables members of a minority group or members of a combination of minority groups to make a meaningful impact on the organization in which they participate. As suggested by the National Advisory Commission on Civil Disorders, the curriculum and other aspects of school are affected by who is in charge (National Advisory Commission on Civil Disorders 1968:436–37). Thus, all of the Black members of the School Committee asked to be appointed to the superintendent's Search Committee. They and the individuals of color already appointed produced a critical mass for minority representation. And they had an effect. With new kinds of people on the Search Committee and the School Committee, and new kinds of people in charge as officers, behold the Boston School Committee did a new thing!

There was no need to wrestle with the long, drawn-out approach of changing attitudes so that discriminatory practices eventually could be changed. With changes in the kinds of people who served on the School Committee, changes in its customs and ways of doing business were immediate. The most fundamental and immediate change was the election of the first African American as superintendent of the Boston public schools.

It was, in part, because more than one-third of the members of the Search Committee were African American or Latinos that the list of finalists for the Office of Superintendent consisted of a Black educator with extensive experience in school administration and urban education, a Latino educator with extensive experience in urban and bilingual education, and a White educator with extensive experience in school administration and higher education. If the Search Committee had consisted exclusively of the kinds of people who served on the School Committee before the era of school desegregation, it is doubtful that a diversified list of finalists would have emerged. For the first time in its history, the Boston School Committee in 1985 was given the opportunity of appointing a person of color as superintendent. It acted favorably on this opportunity.

Among the Black members of the Search Committee working in behalf of the appointment of Wilson were an officer of the NAACP and two people of color from the School Committee. One Black School Committee member supported the Latino candidate. Another Black School Committee member eventually supported Wilson but was indecisive until the search process was nearly concluded because of Wilson's vacillation on the issue of race. Thus, most of the people of color on the Search Committee (except one Black and one Latino) strongly supported Wilson. The NAACP officer sensed that Wilson had a traditional philosophy of education similar to his own. Therefore, he enthusiastically supported Wilson and lobbied White conservative members on the Search Committee in Wilson's behalf. So while Wilson denied his race as a significant factor in the school superintendency contest, his selection, in part, was a consequence of the overwhelming support he received from people of color and the White business community.

Cornel West has counseled Black leaders against becoming so obsessed with white racism that they are unable to effect social change by means of broadly based alliances (West 1994:99). The Blacks in Boston understood this principle well. They made alliances with Whites, Latinos, and the chair of the School Committee who was of Italian ancestry, to obtain the votes necessary for Wilson's election. Black political action in Boston, which resulted in the appointment of the first Black superintendent of schools, demonstrates that, without deliberately forging alliances and building coalitions, a minority candidate was not likely to prevail. High on the agenda of community education for all racial and ethnic minority groups should be teaching and learning how, when, and under what conditions alliances should be made and coalitions formed. To make appropriate alliances, one must understand that "the black freedom struggle is a matter of ethical principles *and* wise politics" (emphasis added) (West 1994:38); which is to say, as Cornel West does, "Blackness is a political and ethical construct" (West 1994:39).

Wilson's reluctance to embrace race as a significant factor in his candidacy might be a function of his definition of race as a biological construct, an error that the public often makes, but one that the Blacks in Boston did not make. They insisted that the Search Committee be comprised of more people of color, but they did not insist that all people of color must think and act the same way. Of some of the Blacks on the Search Committee, one served as an officer of the committee and was solidly for Wilson, another lobbied White conservatives in behalf of Wilson's candidacy; still another made investigative trips to communities in which Wilson had worked to take soundings on his inclination to seek what is in the best interest of Blacks. Finally, one of the Black School Committee members decided to vote for the Latino candidate, declaring that Wilson was too conservative. In Boston, racial and ethnic minorities were not essentialists; they did not make skin color and ethnicity the fundamental issues. They engaged in moral reasoning regarding an ethical outcome that a candidate with a background different from others who had led the school system in the past, and with a background similar to that of most of the students enrolled should have a chance to try to turn the system around, since others had tried with only modest success. If Wilson could not do this, Boston Blacks would not continue to support him.

Moreover, Wilson did not create an obligatory relationship between himself and the Black community, since he downplayed race as a significant factor in his candidacy. According to the moral reasoning of Blacks, they tend to withhold esteem from any leader, including a Black leader, who does not make upgrading the Black community from its experience of racial oppression a high priority (Willie 1986). Such, they believe, is a matter of justice. Thus, one can understand why some Blacks were lukewarm toward Wilson's candidacy after his refusal to play the race card and because of his traditional administrative style. Nevertheless, they put their trust in him. In the end, they were confounded.

In fairness to Wilson, we infer that he believed a school system competently administered so that it helps all children in the end will help minority children, too. Thus, early on, he gave his administration the task of developing a comprehensive educational plan for Boston. Plans for the student body as a whole are frequently inadequate to deal with the special needs of particular subgroup populations, a fact that apparently was not sufficiently reflected in Wilson's planning models.

Wilson came into office with firm support from the business community. Nobel Prize–winning economist, W. Arthur Lewis, an educator and public administrator, tells us that patronage is not sufficient (quoted in Willie 1986). It will vanish. The goodwill of the business leaders began to vanish soon, as Wilson spent a good portion of his "honeymoon" period studying the school system rather than taking swift actions of reform.

The striking feature of Wilson's study of the school system is that it sought to involve the whole community (more than three hundred task force members) and truly was intended to be a consensus operation. After amassing scores of recommendations from his citizens' planning groups, Wilson abandoned his democratic consensus-oriented approach and became quite autocratic in determining which of the recommendations he would present to the School Committee for implementation. Some citizens who participated in the democratic planning process turned against Wilson as he moved into his top-down mode of decision making. Even some of his business supporters accused him of being too bureaucratic and running a ship too centralized with top-down decision making. Wilson bristled at these criticisms and continued in his traditional pattern as the hard-driving, hard-working, hands-on executive deeply enmeshed in and knowledgeable about every aspect of the school system. Wilson was rightfully annoyed at some of the criticisms because they seemed to ignore several improvements in the school system that occurred during his administration.

As student achievement scores, which Wilson promised to increase, continued to lag, business leaders became impatient. Wilson was so traditional in his approach to education that he never discussed a redefinition of indicators of achievement with the business community, indicators other than test scores. Actually, the business community projected onto Wilson much of its displeasure with the School Committee, which frequently meddled in administrative matters to the detriment of all and neglected its policymaking responsibilities. Also, business leaders and political leaders were unhappy with the budget-breaking practices of the school system.

Despite Wilson's hard-working style, some members of the School Committee expressed displeasure with him and began to demonstrate their displeasure by pointing to financial incidents, such as Wilson's alleged misuse of a corporate credit card. The actual amount of money involved was minuscule when compared to the multimillion-dollar budget that he managed for the Boston public schools. Insignificant matters like the credit card were pounced on, especially since Wilson was the only city administrator who carried a corporate credit card. Even the mayor of Boston had not been granted this privilege.

Part of Wilson's failure to take decisive action was because he did not effectively delegate authority despite his hierarchical orientation. Thus, he frequently had too many issues on his plate and only a limited amount of time to deal with them because of his desire to be deeply involved in all decisions. Moreover, Wilson's bureaucratic mode, according to one Black commentator, caused him to be "abrasive." This, in turn, "turned off even those School Committee members who wanted to work with him" (Beaumont 1993:172).

As Wilson's business patrons and the conservative School Committee members who supported him slowly turned against him, his support became increasingly race based. Such support was not enthusiastic, however, since Wilson had distanced himself from advocating racial minority concerns early in his administration. Wilson eventually recognized as a mistake his failure to cultivate more consistent and wholehearted relations with the Black community. By then, however, it was too late to recapture this lost opportunity.

Finally, one of the conservative White members of the School Committee, Dan Burke, who once had been Wilson's ally, was elected chair of the School Committee, and he turned against Wilson. After four years, Wilson's more liberal White friends on the School Committee moved on to other interests and did not seek re-election. Here again, patronage alone would not be enough to save Wilson, a lesson that all public administrators should learn. The Black votes on the School Committee were insufficient to save him. Because some of the criticisms against Wilson appeared to be thinly veiled racial attacks, all four Black members of the School Committee continued to support him. They did not, however, lobby their colleagues for support as they had done when Wilson was hired. The Black community did not protest when Wilson was dismissed.

In 1990, five years after he was hired as Boston's first Black superintendent, or the first superintendent who happened to be Black (the latter label which Wilson clearly preferred), Wilson was dismissed. The Black School Committee members made perfunctory noises of disagreement over Wilson's dismissal. But they did not fully embrace Wilson's dismissal as a "Black cause" in the end since he had failed to fully embrace Blacks as an "administrator's cause" in the beginning.

The limitations of the Wilson administration are frequently mentioned. Unfortunately, less attention has been given to many of Wilson's positive accomplishments. Today, Wilson still believes and says that his administration demonstrated "that a Black man can be an effective Chief Executive Officer" although he steadfastly believed as well that "race should have no part to play in who . . . leads an organization" (Wilson interview, April 19, 1996).

Following Wilson's term as superintendent of schools, Boston's next permanent superintendent of schools was a Black woman educator. So it may be argued that the competent way that Wilson served the community opened the door for other racial minority executives to occupy the office of superintendent of public schools in Boston.

Because of his fine education, strong executive skills, and extensive experience, Wilson remained in office five years. Prior to his appointment in 1985, Boston had gone through eight superintendents in thirteen years. Thus, Wilson helped stabilize this office, a process that his predecessor, Robert Spillane, had begun during his four-year term. During his time in office, Wilson claims that student dropout and suspension rates declined. Also during this tenure, Black individuals were appointed for the first time to positions as facilities director, food services director and police chief of the Boston public schools, and a Puerto Rican was appointed director of bilingual education. The zone superintendent for secondary education, appointed by Wilson, was a person of Asian background.

Educationally, Wilson introduced several Early Learning Centers, which were well received. The President's Award for Excellence in Education was given to the Timilty Middle School in Boston because of its creative program which featured Saturday and after-school classes; this program was introduced by Wilson when he took charge of the school system in 1985. Finally, Wilson implemented the first year of the Controlled Choice student assignment plan in Boston, which successfully provided 90 percent of the students their first- or second-choice school. This system has eliminated "forced busing" in Boston and led to the desegregation of all elementary and middle schools. During Wilson's administration, the school system aggressively sought money from the federal government for magnet schools. The Boston public schools were awarded grants in excess of $5 million.

Despite the good that he achieved, Wilson was not able to fully implement his extensive vision for educational improvement for the City of Boston. His sixteen-point plan received a national award for excellence as a strategic plan but was never implemented the way that Wilson had planned and would have preferred. While Wilson believed his record spoke for itself, he was among the first to acknowledge that "a great deal more improvement is needed" in the Boston public schools. However, he along with Robert Spillane prepared a good foundation for the future.

The Wilson administration provides important lessons about community organization and conflict resolution. Reconciling opposites is one of the most important responsibilities of a public administrator. Finding ways to harmonize disparate interests into educational plans and policies that work for all are central, challenging responsibilities. To accomplish these goals, however, plans for remediation, maintenance, and new opportunities may have to be implemented in specific ways for different population groups whose needs are not the same.

Among the disparate interest groups in urban communities that must be reconciled, race stands out. Wilson tried to rise above racial considerations in the policies that he recommended and promoted. His self-description as a superintendent who happened to be Black illustrates his belief that race, if considered at all, should be secondary in leadership and public policymaking decisions.

Yet, racial matters contributed to the premature termination of Wilson's superintendency in Boston. The White business interest groups embraced Wilson initially because of his advertised fiscal conservatism. When they withdrew support, racial and ethnic minority populations did not rush in to defend him. Thus, in the end, Wilson stood alone with little support from racial minority and majority interest groups, and his superintendency was rejected.

The Wilson story teaches us that public administrators must learn how to work through the conflicts and confrontations of all racial, ethnic, socioeconomic, and other interest groups equitably. This is the essence of good public administration.

Reflecting upon his time in Boston five years after he resigned, Wilson still believes that he was right to attempt to be a superintendent for all of the students.

He acknowledged that he had some difficulty with the Latino population because of a remark he made about why its members should learn to speak English. He continued to believe that getting too close to one Black leader who had challenged the mayor in an earlier election might have aggravated the process of maintaining a positive relationship with the mayor. From his perspective, business support remained with him to the end. Others report that his business support diminished.

Wilson said that the superintendent cannot relate to the whole community as frequently as some people would like. Community superintendents are needed to meet and work with the community. Wilson said that a superintendent of a large school system should have a policy adviser on his or her staff to reach out and inform the political system. We would agree and would also suggest that a superintendent, Black, Brown, or White, who is superintendent for all of the students should have a minority affairs adviser to stay connected with various racial and ethnic populations.

From the analysis of this case study two conclusions are emphasized: (1) race continues to be significant in educational matters; and (2) staking one's future on a single power source in the community is a questionable practice for survival.

While the first Black superintendent of schools in Boston preferred to be identified as a superintendent who happened to be Black, clearly more was at stake in his appointment than the content of his character. In his appointment, Boston was trying to clean up its tarnished image that resulted from violent clashes between White and Black students following the school desegregation court order. New players were emerging on the political field as the Irish lock on local political offices began to weaken. Among the new players were individuals of Italian, Latino, and African American ethnicity. Together, these groups had power; singly they did not. Under these circumstances, race and ethnicity mattered in ways that go beyond concern about the competency of school leaders. One ignores these contextual facts at one's own peril.

Business has always been a big player in local community affairs. However, no interest group is strong enough to go it alone, not even business. Coalitions are needed, but the winning coalition is not always the same; from time to time, it changes. Because of this, any administrator should recognize the danger of relying on only one sector of the community. Linkage with several power groups is essential if one wishes to survive. The ability to reconcile opposites by finding common ground between disparate support groups is an essential qualification for leaders in public administration, including school superintendents.

REFERENCES

Beaumont, Jennifer. 1993. "Factors Contributing to Involuntary Superintendency Turnover in Urban Public School Systems." Unpublished doctoral dissertation, University of Maryland, Baltimore County.

Citywide Educational Coalitions. *BPS in Brief.* December 1987; August 1988.

Dahl, Robert A. 1967. *Pluralist Democracy in the United States.* Chicago: Rand McNally.

Edwards, Ralph. 1989. "How Boston Selected Its First Black Superintendent of Schools." Unpublished doctoral dissertation, Harvard Graduate School of Education, Cambridge, MA.

National Advisory Commission on Civil Disorders. 1968. *Report.* Washington DC: U.S. Government Printing Office.

Schrag, Peter. 1967. *Village School Downtown.* Boston: Beacon Press.

Smith, Ralph R. 1978. "Two Centuries and Twenty-Four Months: A Chronicle of the Struggle to Desegregate the Boston Public Schools." In Howard I. Kalodner and James Fishman (eds.), *Limits of Justice.* Pp. 25–113. Cambridge, MA: Ballinger.

West, Cornel. 1994. *Race Matters.* New York: Vintage.

Willie, Charles V. 1978. *The Sociology of Urban Education.* Lexington, MA: Lexington Books.

Willie, Charles V. 1984. *School Desegregation Plans that Work.* Westport, CT: Greenwood Press.

Willie, Charles V. 1986. *Five Black Scholars.* Lanham, MD: University Press of America and Abt Books.

Wilson, Laval. April 19, 1996. Interview by authors at Harvard University.

U.S. Bureau of the Census. 1960. *Statistical Abstract of the United States.* Washington, DC: U.S. Government Printing Office.

U.S. Bureau of the Census. 1994. *Statistical Abstract of the United States.* Washington, DC: U.S. Government Printing Office.

3. _____ The Case of an Elected Versus an Appointed School Committee

In July 1991 Governor William Weld of Massachusetts signed a bill that abolished Boston's thirteen-member elected school committee and replaced it with a seven-member school board that would be appointed by the mayor. Enactment of this legislation was considered a victory for the city's mayor and business community who had fought hard to achieve it. But among African Americans, the new law was generally regarded as a setback.

For Mayor Raymond Flynn the legislation meant he would now gain control over the one city agency that did not report directly to him. For Boston's business community, it satisfied their goal of transferring responsibility for the city's schools from what many considered a dysfunctional school board to a chief executive who could be held accountable for the schools' performance. As this study will show, Boston's business community became increasingly involved in reforming the city's school system, where student achievement was consistently low.

For African Americans, however, the legislation had broader, more political implications. Since *Morgan vs. Hennigan*, Boston's landmark 1974 school desegregation case, education had been the city's primary arena for Black political empowerment. Indeed, in 1991, when the new legislation was signed, four Blacks were serving on the elected school committee and two had been elected at-large. By contrast, there were

---

This chapter was written with the assistance of Lisa Gonsalves.

only two African Americans on the thirteen-member City Council, and neither held an at-large seat. Abolishing the elected school committee, therefore, removed four of the city's six elected Black officials and left African Americans with no at-large representation in city government.

Boston's public schools, moreover, had become overwhelmingly non-White (80%) since desegregation, and most of the system's students of color were Black. In 1985, Boston's elected school committee appointed the city's first African American superintendent of schools and, upon dismissing him in 1990, selected a Black woman as his replacement. For all of these reasons, the elected school committee was politically as well as educationally important to African Americans in Boston, and most did not want to lose it.

This case study examines the process through which that loss occurred. It will focus mainly on the efforts of the mayor and business community to attain an appointed school board and the manner in which Black community interests opposed or supported those efforts. We selected this focus because while other municipal forces had some impact in this case (and we will cite where this occurred), our research has identified the mayor, the city's business community, and Boston's African American leadership as the event's principal protagonists. Accordingly, our study will try to answer these two key questions:

1. What were the main contributing factors to the mayor's and business community's success in obtaining an appointed school committee?
2. In what manner did Boston's African American leadership oppose or support efforts to create such a committee?

We begin with a brief review of the business community's involvement in Boston's public schools. Tracing that involvement will also help to illuminate the importance of Boston's school desegregation experience for understanding the case before us.

Prior to 1975, when Phase II of the plan to desegregate Boston's schools began, the business community was essentially a bystander in the city's school desegregation struggle. Much has been written about *Morgan vs. Hennigan*, the case that precipitated that struggle (see, for example, Lucas 1985; Murningham 1984; Ross and Berg 1981) so we won't comment at length upon it here. One should take note, however, of how ten years of the federal court's presence in Boston's schools transformed the city's social climate.

The federal judge in the case, W. Arthur Garrity, found in his June 21, 1974, decision that "The entire school system of Boston is unconstitutionally segregated." That fall, Garrity implemented Phase I of his desegregation plan, whose most controversial feature called for busing Black students in to South Boston, a predominantly White, working-class section of the city (Lucas 1985).

This strategy led to several physical attacks on the Black students, intervention by the police and state militias, and sensational national coverage by the media, which brought disrepute to the city. During this period, the Boston School Committee, several prominent White leaders (including some elected officials), and segments of the White population angrily opposed the court's intervention. Indeed, over the course of the case, Judge Garrity issued over four-hundred separate court orders to force compliance with desegregation mandates. This was not a period when noticeable support for the court's role was forthcoming from most municipal sectors, including the business community.

But in May 1975, when Phase II of the plan was introduced, much of this changed. While busing continued under Phase II, the court also introduced plans to create partnerships between the public schools and the city's universities and business institutions. Initially, the business community's participation consisted of providing summer jobs for Boston's high school students.

In 1980, an especially successful summer jobs program was conducted by the Private Industry Council (PIC), a consortium of prominent business organizations created the previous year to supervise Boston's publicly funded employment programs. That fall PIC initiated a year-round education and employment program called the Jobs Collaborative, and this program also ran well (Edwards 1989).

These successes led, in 1982, to the signing of the first Boston Compact. The compact is an agreement between the city's schools and business organizations in which the latter promise to provide jobs for students and the former agree to meet specified academic goals. By 1985, at least 350 companies had joined the compact, while PIC's summer programs continued to run smoothly. Although the system's academic gains have generally failed to match agreed-upon standards, the compact has been regularly renewed and continues to function today.

Also currently functioning is the Boston Plan for Excellence, which was launched in 1984 with a $1.5 million gift from the Bank of Boston. Funds provided through this program are used to support teacher development, provide student scholarships, and pay for academic and athletic programs in the city's schools (Edwards 1989).

Once they began to invest at this level in the city's public schools, Boston business interests also started to more closely examine how the schools were being managed. This drew their attention immediately to the Boston School Committee, which even before its desegregation problems had been criticized for inefficiency, patronage, and narrowness of public access (Schrag 1967).

The desegregation experience had begun to address the issue of access, however. Indeed, the city as a whole seemed to be seeking a more liberal persona late in the desegregation period. This was reflected, in part, by the election, for the first time, of an African American (John O'Bryant) to the five-member, at-large School Committee in 1978. In 1981, O'Bryant was joined on the committee by another Black, Jean McGuire. And, in 1983, when the committee was expanded to thirteen members (nine representing districts, four elected at-large) four Blacks won seats in that year's election. Since that time, there have always been four Blacks on the thirteen–member School Committee.

As a policymaking body, however, the thirteen-member committee proved no more effective than its five-member predecessor. From the beginning it found itself immobilized by internal strife, policy failures, and leadership conflicts with its superintendents (Edwards 1989). In addition, the new committee continued to preside over a lethargic, in-bred school bureaucracy that had flourished for decades under the five-member boards (Schrag 1967).

For some time the business community had been concerned with how the Boston School Committee functioned. As early as 1972, the Boston Municipal Research Bureau (BMRB) had proposed that a clearer separation of roles be established between the superintendent and the School Committee. BMRB is the city's leading fiscal "watchdog" organization and is strongly influenced by business interests. In its monitoring role, BMRB had concluded that the School Committee had too much authority in personnel matters and was too prone to micro-manage the school system. The superintendent, it felt, should have clearer responsibility for the system's day-to-day operations, with the School Committee confining itself exclusively to matters of policy (Interview with Sam Tyler, Director of the Boston Municipal Research Bureau, 1993).

In 1978, BMRB sought to achieve these goals by working with School Committee president John Finnigan. When this proved unsuccessful, it proposed that the problems be addressed through legislation. Largely through BMRB efforts, three bills were filed, over time, in the Massachusetts state legislature.

The Trager bill in 1982 was designed to give the superintendent ultimate authority over all School Department personnel. However, the bill was defeated, partly through the opposition of the teachers' union. In 1986, a bill did pass. This one defined the budget responsibilities of the School Department and strengthened the superintendent's budgetary role.

Finally, in 1987, Chapter 613 was enacted. This law dramatically strengthened the superintendent's role by transferring practically all personnel matters from the School Committee to the office of the superintendent. Prior to this, the School Committee's responsibility in personnel matters included the hiring and firing of school staff, at all levels. Chapter 613's supporters hoped that the School Committee would now attend exclusively to policy matters and leave the administration of the system to the superintendent.

This failed to occur, however, and, at the behest of the business community, BMRB began to explore possible options in governance. In 1987 it produced a survey that compared the structure and operation of school boards in twenty-five large urban systems. Based upon the survey's information, business leaders attempted to broker changes in the School Committee's operation through a consensus among the committee's leadership, top city officials, and themselves.

They brought together the School Committee's officers; the mayor himself and his director of administrative services; and a representative from the "Vault," an informal organization of top business executives who meet periodically around municipal issues. One notes immediately the elitist and all-White nature of this group. There was not one minority person among them, although the superintendent and several School Committee members were Black, and a majority of the school system's students were minorities.

The consensus obtained by this group, after meeting for several months during 1987, was that site-based management would be a system-wide priority and that the School Committee would again be admonished to follow the letter and spirit of Chapter 613. The group's negotiations ended in May 1987.

However, one year later business leaders concluded that the agreement was not working. In the words of Sam Tyler, director of the Boston Municipal Research Bureau, the "elected School Committee still saw itself as politicians whose role was to provide constituency services, which inevitably meant [it] would get involved in daily operations and would tie the superintendent's staff down with work that [had nothing to do with establishing] policy guidelines" (Tyler interview, 1993).

In the meantime, there was general dissatisfaction with the School Committee's performance among parents and other members of the community. One area that particularly concerned them was student assignment. As part of its desegregation program the federal court had designed and monitored the implementation of a student assignment plan since 1974. In 1987, however, the U.S. Court of Appeals declared that Boston was free to create new student assignment guidelines, provided they did not resegregate the system. Here was a chance, many felt, to create school choice options and to reduce the traveling time for many students. But the School Committee took little action on this opportunity. It merely created a two person subcommittee on the matter, which did no more than hold an exploratory meeting with a consultant.

The superintendent at this time was Laval Wilson who, upon his appointment in 1985, had become the first African American to hold the position. Dr. Wilson had included student assignment among the areas to be studied by several task forces he created in 1986 to assist him in developing a strategic plan for Boston's schools. Wilson's student assignment task force made recommendations to him based upon the federal court's original plan. And it was those recommendations that Wilson advised the School Committee to follow, notwithstanding the appeals court's decision. But the School Committee neither acted on Dr. Wilson's recommendations nor instructed him to change them.

This inaction on the School Committee's part prompted several parents and community organizations (including the NAACP, the Urban League, and the teachers' union) to express their dissatisfaction in a strongly worded March 8, 1988, memorandum to the School

Committee. The School Committee's response was to propose a series of hearings on the matter that would extend into August. Dissatisfied with this plan, several parents and community members turned to Mayor Flynn for help.

After meeting with them, Flynn agreed to hire consultants who would work with the community to develop a new assignment plan. The mayor's consultants, Charles Willie and Michael Alves, an inter-racial team, connected with Harvard University, began their work in July 1988, although the School Committee went ahead with its hearings. The mayor, in effect, had set in motion an alternative method of developing a student assignment plan. Nevertheless, the School Committee eventually agreed with the plan developed by his consultants and ratified it in February 1989. It was during this period, however, when parents and community leaders turned to him out of frustration with the School Committee, that the mayor first took action that would eventually lead to the elected committee's removal.

His first formal step was to create a panel in October 1988 called the Special Advisory Committee on School Reform. Flynn charged the committee to develop specific recommendations for him in five key areas: school-based management, school governance, school facilities, student assignment, and values in the school curriculum. The Committee was racially diverse and included high-ranking representatives from various sectors of the community.

The chair was Hubie Jones, an African American and Boston University's dean of social work. Other African Americans of note on the committee were City Councillor Bruce Bolling, School Committee member Juanita Wade, and Franklyn Jennifer, chancellor of the State Board of Higher Education. Among Whites on the committee were Ferdinand Colleredo-Mansfield, chairman of the "Vault"; William Edgerly of State Street Bank; and Edward Doherty, president of the Boston Teachers' Union. There were also four parents and community representatives on the committee: one White, one Black, and two Latinos.

This group endorsed the student assignment plan (called "controlled choice") prepared by the mayor's consultants well before the School Committee did so. It then turned its attention to school governance, which was a mayoral priority. BMRB shared with the Special Advisory Committee both its "study" of urban school systems and the 1987 "agreement" among the mayor, business leaders, and the school committee's officers.

In January 1988 the Advisory Committee's recommendations were released through the media, although its written report would not be made public until several months later. The one recommendation that was highlighted in the report, and seized upon by the media, was that the Boston School Committee should be appointed by the mayor. Little attention was given in the release or by the media to the other areas the Advisory Committee had been charged to consider.

A few weeks later Boston's City Council passed an ordinance authorizing it to create a similar panel, called the Special Commission on Public Education. The Special Commission's membership was announced in May 1989, two days after the Special Advisory Committee's official report was made public. Media coverage of the report continued to emphasize the issue of governance. For example, the city's leading newspaper, the *Boston Globe*, captioned its news story on the document: "Report Calls for Appointed School Board" (May 1, 1989). The accompanying article focused on that particular recommendation alone.

The seven-person Special Commission was selected and announced by Mayor Flynn. Like his Advisory Committee, the commission's membership was also racially diverse and prestigious. The chair was James Jennings, an African American and head of the African American Studies Department at the University of Massachusetts in Boston. African American city councillor Bruce Bolling, who had served on the Special Advisory Committee, was also named to the Special Commission. The commission's other African American member was Loretta Roach, executive director of the Citywide Educational Coalition (CWEC), Boston's leading school oversight organization.

There was one Asian on the commission, Dang Pham of the Bilingual Parents Advisory Council; one Latino, Juan Tapia of the Citywide Parents Council; and two Whites, City Council president Michael McCormack and Cynthia Politch from the Special Needs Advisory Council.

While the commission, like its predecessor, was charged to study a range of educational issues (e.g., dropout rates, test scores), Mayor Flynn was quite explicit this time about his governance priority. He directed the commission to immediately focus on the school committee and "recommend a course of action within 30 days in order to preserve the option of placing a referendum question before the people this fall" (from the commission's final report).

The commission scheduled public hearings on the matter for the end of May and early June, but before the hearings had even ended, Flynn announced that he intended to seek a referendum on the status of the elected school board. At the hearings, almost everyone who testified expressed dissatisfaction with the current School Committee and agreed that a change was needed. However, only a small minority of the approximately 120 people who attended supported an all-appointed school board.

Because of this the commission proposed two school board structures in its July 1989 report. One called for a nine-person board comprised of both elected and appointed members; the other proposed a seven-member, all-appointed school committee. BMRB immediately criticized the half-elected/half appointed option and released its 1987 urban school boards "study" to the media. Then, on August 9, Mayor Flynn held a press conference (at school committee headquarters) where he unveiled the referendum question he planned for the November ballot. The question read as follows: "Shall the current 13–member School Committee structure be changed to a new seven-member school board, appointed by the Mayor from a list of Boston residents selected by a nominating panel comprised of parents, educators, community leaders, business and labor leaders?"

At this point, organizations in the Black community opposed to an appointed School Committee had begun to participate in the debate. Foremost among them was the Black Political Task Force. Until the governance controversy, the main role the task force had played was to review and endorse African American candidates running for office. However, the Black Political Task Force's efforts in opposing the appointed school committee were soon widely covered in the local media. The task force appeared to be the major voice of opposition to the appointed board in the Black community. While the task force reacted publicly, a group of Boston's African American and Latino elected officials began to meet privately in order to solidify support for saving the elected school committee.

These meetings, held on Thursday mornings at Bob the Chef's, a Roxbury restaurant, were organized by Mel King, a well-known Black community activist who had been an unsuccessful mayoral candidate in the 1983 election won by Mayor Flynn. Most minority elected officials in Boston attended some of these meetings. They included two officials from the City Council, the four Black members of the elected School Committee, along with the four minority House and Senate members in the state legislature. Except for Bruce Bolling, all of the city's elected minority officials and state representatives were united in their opposition to an appointed board. The African American and Latino elected officials met several times with the Black clergy, some of whom had already stood with Mayor Flynn in support of an appointed board. In these meetings, they attempted to convince the ministers to support the principle of an elected school committee. The meetings were described as open and honest, but the group as a whole was unable to reach a unanimous position on the issue. Some of the ministers, in fact, had strong political ties to the mayor and did not wish to challenge him. Others favored an appointed school committee out of personal conviction.

The leaders of the Black Political Task Force, during the early part of the school committee controversy, were Tony Crayton, president of the task force, and Joyce Ferriabough, communications chair. Ferriabough eventually succeeded Crayton as president and took a somewhat different approach to the issue. She favored consideration of a partly appointed board and this created some confusion within the task force. The task force was unified, however, during its first press conference on the issue. During that press conference, Ferriabough stated that the task force would "take a formal position after interviewing representatives from both sides" (*Boston Globe*, Aug. 16, 1989, p. 33). To start that process, BPTF president Tony Crayton met with Flynn adviser David Cortiella in August to learn more about the mayor's plan. Crayton said that the BPTF was concerned because "we have been fairly hard-pressed to find people in the black community who are in favor of this on its face" (*Boston Globe*, Aug. 16, 1989, p. 33).

Cortiella responded by pointing out that James Jennings, a former Black Political Task Force president, headed the panel that advised Flynn to adopt an appointed school committee. Cortiella noted other prominent African Americans who supported the appointed committee, including Hubert Jones, dean of the Boston University School of Social Work; Franklyn Jennifer, chancellor of Higher Education; Nedra Williams, chairwoman of the Education Committee of the Boston chapter of the NAACP; and Ron Homer, president of the Boston Bank of Commerce. The *Boston Globe*, which published a story about the August meeting, called attention to the split in the Black community. The same article referred to Bruce Bolling (who was chair of the City Council's Education Committee and the only individual to serve on both the mayor's Special Advisory Committee on School Reform and the City Council's Special Commission on Education) as "one of Flynn's most prominent Black supporters on the school issue" (*Boston Globe*, Aug. 16, 1989, p. 33).

In August 1989, Bolling's African American colleague on the Boston City Council, Charles Yancey, introduced an alternative referendum question asking voters to choose between the current thirteen-member board or a smaller, seven-member elected board. Yancey developed the new plan with Black School Committee member John O'Bryant (Charles Yancey interview, 1993).

Yet another referendum question was proposed by City Councillor Rosaria Solerno. Her option kept Mayor Flynn's original question intact, but limited the first term of any appointed board to four years, after which time the voters would get a chance to revisit the issue. The City Council had little more than a month to approve the referendum language in time for the November ballot. All three of the referendum questions (Flynn's, Yancey's, and Salerno's) were referred to the City Council's Committee on Education, chaired by Bolling. The committee decided to hold two public hearings before making a final recommendation.

As chair of the Education Committee, Bolling had the option of recommending to the full council one of the referendum questions, a series of questions, or a single question with various options. About thirty witnesses testified at the hearings, which were held on August 22 and 23, 1989. At these hearings a majority supported an appointed school committee.

Meanwhile, two new groups emerged in the struggle: one supporting an appointed committee, the other opposed. One group, the Better Education Committee, was formed by Mayor Flynn in September 1989 to advocate for an all-appointed school board. The first task of this group was to push for passage of Flynn's referendum question. The committee was made up of forty-six members and reflected the racial and ethnic makeup of the school system. It was chaired by three education activists, Carol Wright, Tony Molina, and George Joe. In its report on the committee's formation, the *Boston Globe* commented:

While some leaders in the city's minority community, which constitute a majority of the public schools' enrollment, have expressed reservations about taking away their right to elect school committee representatives,many [Better Education] committee members are Black, Hispanic or Asian. And the leaders are not just Flynn's political allies. Lloyd King, brother of former State Rep. Melvin H. King, whom Flynn defeated in the 1983 election, is on the committee. Others include Hubie Jones, Dean of the Boston University School of Social Work. (*Boston Globe*, Sept. 12, 1989, p. 26)

While the news story acknowledged the presence of opposition to an appointed school committee in the Black community, it also indicated that several prominent Blacks supported the mayor's proposal.

The other group to emerge that September was the National Association of Black Americans, led by Jack Robinson, former president of Boston's NAACP. This organization announced plans to start a grassroots campaign to fight the proposal for an appointed school committee. Robinson was quoted in the *Boston Globe* as saying, "the Black voting population in Boston is being asked to vote away their vote" (*Boston Globe*, Sept. 12, 1989, p. 26).

Toward the end of September 1989, Bruce Bolling's Education Committee of the City Council recommended a three-option question for the ballot. The question asked voters "whether they support either the current 13-member elected panel, a seven-member panel appointed by the mayor, or a seven-member elected panel that would have its own taxing and spending power," with voter reevaluation after eight years. The City Council approved the new referendum question unanimously, before the deadline for the November ballot.

However, supporters of the appointed school committee in the business community and elsewhere did not let the issue die. They called Mayor Flynn, demanding that he lobby the City Council to vote again on the referendum question. According to Bruce Bolling,

The mayor put . . . a full-court press on the issue. I had never seen any lobbying effort by the mayor that was greater than this effort to get the council to overturn what it had previously done. He fought hard to rescind this. The mayor was influenced by the business community. They were about to leave involvement with the Private Industry Council and pull out of their active role in the Boston Public Schools. The mayor had a lot at stake with the business community on the issue. (Bolling interview, 1993)

The mayor's lobbying effort paid off. The City Council voted 11 to 2 to switch its support from Bolling's language to Flynn's referendum, which required only a "yes" or "no" response. The vote was split along racial lines with Bolling and Yancey, the council's two Black members, voting against the yes-no version. The vote also took place in early October, five days after the September 27 legal deadline for questions to appear on the November ballot. Nevertheless, the final referendum returned to Flynn's original language: "Shall the current 13-member School Committee structure be changed to a new seven-member school board, appointed by the mayor from a list of Boston residents selected by a nominating panel comprised of parents, educators, community leaders, business and labor leaders?" As Bolling saw it, this question did not represent a true choice for the voters. "No one wanted the present 13-member structure," he said. "A real choice would have been between an elected or an appointed committee" (Bolling interview, 1992).

Six days before the election, the *Boston Globe* came out against the appointed school committee and urged a no vote on the referendum question in the state legislature. The *Globe's* main argument for a "no" vote took into consideration the racial and ethnic tensions in Boston politics. The editorial stated, "It is troubling that as the Black community edges toward political power, the now dominant Irish, in alliance with business interests, would try to brake that progress by withdrawing the right to vote for School Committee members" (*Boston Globe*, Nov. 1, 1989, p. 18).

Two days before the election, Flynn and the Better Education Committee allegedly spent $65,000 on television and radio ads in an attempt to persuade the public to vote yes on the referendum question. All in all, it is alleged that the business community contributed approximately $150,000 to the referendum campaign. The money was funneled through the Better Education Committee that sponsored ads, mailings, and "dear-friends" cards (*Boston Globe*, Nov. 4, 1989, p. 26; and Dec. 8, 1989, p. 42). The night before the election, Mayor Flynn released a report critical of the high dropout rate in the Boston public schools. The report gained front-page coverage in election day newspapers.

In Massachusetts, the state legislature must enact a home-rule petition that authorizes civil divisions, like the City of Boston, to change the method of selecting the school committee. Mayor Flynn

lieved that the legislature might not act on a home-
..hnout a clear signal from the referendum outcome
Globe, Sept. 20, 1989, p. 35). Mayor Flynn and supporters of the
appointed school committee won their fight over the wording of the
referendum question. In the end, however, they did not get a clear
voter mandate. The "yes" vote in the November referendum won by
a "razor-thin" margin. Of the 56,098 people who voted in the referendum, 28,719 voted for the question and 28,049 voted against it, giving
the supporters a 670 vote lead, which translates to a 50.6 percent to
49.4 percent victory. Twenty thousand more city residents did not
respond negatively or positively to the referendum question. They did
not vote on it.

According to City Councillor Charles Yancey, "The margin of victory for the question came from communities without children. The
Black communities of Roxbury, Mattapan and Dorchester voted
against it along with South Boston, East Boston and Charlestown, the
areas with a majority of kids in the schools" (Yancey interview, 1992).
The *Boston Globe* supported Yancey's assessment. It reported that
"South Boston voted against the question by [a ratio] approaching
2–1. In addition East Boston and Charlestown voted by sizable mar-
gins against the proposal. . . it also lost [by the same margins] in the
heart of Boston's Black community, Wards 9 and 12 in Roxbury and
Ward 14 in Dorchester" (*Boston Globe*, Nov. 8, 1989, p. 1).

As the weeks after the election wore on, it became apparent to
Mayor Flynn that getting his school committee proposal through the
state legislature would be an uphill battle. In a letter sent to Boston
public school parents toward the end of December 1989, Mayor Flynn
stated that he would "not proceed with a home-rule petition . . .
[based on] the referendum's narrow victory" (*Boston Globe*, Dec. 30,
1989, p. 21). He expressed doubt that the state legislature would
support the change without greater local support.

By the end of 1989, Flynn had given up the fight for an appointed
School Committee. However, 1990 became one of the most "trouble-
some" years in the School Committee's experience since the desegregation case. The first half of the year was marked by one controversy
after another. First came the firing of superintendent Laval Wilson in
February; next the committee secretly approved salary increases for
its own staff in the midst of a budget crisis, then rescinded the raises
when the action became public and received a negative response. The

committee's inability to cut the school budget from $409.1 million to the $389.8 million allocated by the city prevented it from having a budget for fiscal 1991 approved on time. Finally, the committee failed to hire a new superintendent to replace Laval Wilson in a timely fashion. All of this seriously discredited the committee at a critical moment.

Nevertheless, the issue of school governance was not raised publicly again until seven months into the year. The City Council took the lead this time. Mayor Flynn stayed out of the process because some City Council members thought his presence was harmful to their cause during the previous struggle. Councillor Michael McCormack said at the time, "The mayor's non-involvement is good. Last year a lot of the votes were directed at Flynn personally" (*Boston Globe*, Aug. 16, 1990, p. 36). The council's plan was to propose a new home-rule petition that would call for a change in school governance; but unlike the previous question, the new petition would be a binding referendum. In order for the question to be binding, it would have to be approved by the state legislature before it went to the voters. This opened the debate about school reform to a new round of players, namely, state representatives and senators, and provided another opportunity for minority community leaders to mobilize around the issue.

Mayor Flynn, however, did reenter the debate at this point. He organized a meeting between City Council and legislative members in September 1990 at the Parkman House, a city-owned conference facility in Boston. The meeting was attended by Mayor Flynn, all the City Councillors, and Democratic representatives Kevin Fitzgerald, Nelson Merced (Dorchester), Byron Rushing (South End), and John McDonough (Jamaica Plain). All four representatives expressed their willingness to compromise and support a half-elected, half-appointed school board. This special meeting was different from earlier negotiating sessions because it was multiracial. Representatives Merced and Rushing, both African Americans with inner-city constituents, stressed the need for other reforms in addition to school governance. Merced, for example, was interested in a plan that would give parents and teachers more power to hire principals. He indicated at the meeting that he would not support a referendum unless it included other reforms (*Boston Globe*, Sept. 5, 1990, p. 21). The deadline to place a binding referendum question on the November ballot, however, was October 1, less than a month away.

After the special meeting of city and state officers, the City Council held a public hearing on school governance at the Roxbury Boy's Club. The hearing was attended by African American voters who voiced strong support for a half-elected, half-appointed school committee (*Boston Globe*, Sept. 7, 1990, p. 19). This meeting demonstrated that a shift had occurred in African American voter sentiment about school governance. Members of the minority community were increasingly willing to accept a half-elected, half-appointed committee; there seemed to be consensus among state legislators for it; and the City Council seemed willing to compromise and endorse it.

Business leadership, however, opposed the emerging consensus. The Boston Municipal Research Bureau released a report written by Samuel Tyler criticizing the half-elected, half-appointed option. In it, he warned that a half-elected, half-appointed panel "would not solve any of [the] school system's management problems" (*Boston Globe*, Sept. 10, 1990, p. 17). The report recommended the option that Mayor Flynn had fought for in 1989, a seven-member school board appointed by the mayor from a nominating panel's recommendations. On the same day, the *Boston Globe* endorsed an all-appointed school panel. The *Globe* editorial stated, "There is a growing consensus for a mixed appointed and elected School Committee. We urge the City Council to consider seriously an all-appointed committee" (*Boston Globe*, Sept. 10, 1990, p. 14). Both the Boston Municipal Research Bureau's report and the *Globe*'s editorial appeared on the first day of school, September 10, 1990.

Meanwhile, the City Council and Mayor Flynn were still trying to work out a compromise with the legislature before the ballot deadline. At this point, the referendum was being held up by the Black legislative delegation who wanted any governance change tied to school management reform and the creation of parent councils. Representative Nelson Merced, for example, wanted the home-rule petition to "include the creation of parent school boards that would have the power to hire principals and set budgets. . . . Whether we have an appointed board or an elected board is irrelevant," he said, "If the home rule petition does not include real school reform, then it shouldn't be on the ballot."

Finally, a compromise was reached. The City Council approved 10 to 2, a home-rule petition for the November ballot that called for a nine-member school committee with five members elected from district and four members appointed by the mayor. African American City Councillor Charles Yancey opposed the measure because he felt that seven members should be elected and two appointed. However, African American City Councillor Bruce Bolling supported the compromise. While the City Council was achieving consensus on a compromise, splits were still revealed in the African American community as indicated by the different stances taken by these two well-respected Black members of the City Council.

Now it was up to the full legislature. The City Council had spent all of its time working with the House of Representatives. No one was quite sure what the Senate would do. There was reason for concern because the Senate president was quoted as saying he would be more likely to support a plan that included school choice, a provision that would allow parents to send their children to any school within the state.

What many had feared then happened. The school committee proposal was killed in the Senate. Some critics blamed Representative Merced's insistence on adding the parent councils for the loss. That part of the measure offended the Boston Teacher's Union because the parent councils excluded teachers. The BTU also felt the parent councils would compete with the school-site councils that had been mandated in the new teachers' contract as part of school-based management. Senator Bill Owens, the only African American in the Senate, also spoke against the measure because he felt it was a denial of the right to vote. Owens's opposition was key in defeating the proposal.

Two months passed, and in early December, Black Political Task Force members met with Mayor Flynn at the Parkman House to present an alternative proposal for school governance. However, the split within the task force had grown, causing it to appear disunited. Some believe that the lack of unity at this meeting encouraged Flynn to ignore the task force's demands.

To fortify opposition to an appointed board, Senator Bill Owens and other African Americans organized a group called the Right to Vote. However, some in the African American community felt that the efforts of this new group were hampered by its refusal to work with Whites who were also opposed to the appointed board.

In December 1990, the City Council voted 10 to 3 in favor of a home-rule petition to abolish the School Committee and place control of the schools directly under Mayor Flynn and the City Council. The petition was supported by the Vault, Boston's most influential business group. Flynn signed the measure and forwarded it to the State Legislature and governor for approval.

This move came after another embarrassment in the School Committee's nine-month search for a new superintendent of schools. John Murphy, a highly qualified semifinalist, dropped out of the process because of the School Committee's poor handling of the search, especially its inability to respect the confidentiality of negotiations. The School Committee was also ridiculed for not balancing its $389.5 million budget.

The City Council's two Black members voted against this latest petition, which the City Council approved in December 1990. Their opposition almost guaranteed another racially polarized fight at the state legislative level because several members of the Black delegation, including Representatives Byron Rushing, Nelson Merced, and Gloria Fox, and Senator Bill Owens had already come out publicly against the bill.

The opposing factions in the dispute took action early in 1991. The task force created an ad hoc coalition to protect Boston's public schools and staged a demonstration in February 1991 at City Hall to protest the home-rule petition, which aimed to abolish the School Committee. The task force also proposed a new referendum question calling for a nine-member half-elected, half-appointed school committee. This proposal was different from one put forth earlier by Tony Crayton, its former president, who had strongly favored an all-elected board.

Meanwhile, the City Council and representatives from the state legislature's Joint Committee on Education began negotiating a compromise between the City Council's bill to abolish the School Committee and those who opposed such a move, namely leaders of the minority community. The following agreement was reached: If the City Council would drop its petition to abolish the School Committee, the legislature's Joint Committee on Education would support a seven-member all-appointed board. The committee's chairmen, Representative Mark Roosevelt and Senator Thomas Birmingham, wrote a letter suggesting this to the City Council in March 1991. This compromise clearly eliminated the half-elected, half-appointed option that had gained increasing support in the African American and Hispanic communities. The City Council submitted two proposals in response to the legislators' letter. The first, filed by Michael McCormack, mirrored the legislators' suggestion for an all-appointed board. However, the two African American city councillors, Bruce Bolling and Charles Yancey, opposed this measure. Bolling submitted a competing proposal calling for a nine-member half-elected, half-appointed board; "After three years of debate . . . it's clear to me . . . that people want to maintain some elected component to the School Committee" (*Boston Globe*, Mar. 26, 1991, p. 30).

A third group, the state's Black Legislative Caucus, opposed all of the proposals that were then on the table. It criticized the Joint Education Committee's recommendation at a state House news conference. According to Bill Owens, a member of the State Education Committee, Co-chairs Roosevelt and Birmingham acted improperly by "recommending the creation of an all-appointed board without a vote" (*Boston Globe*, Mar. 27, 1991, p. 26) by the entire committee. At the same news conference, Representative Nelson Merced, then chair of the caucus, said, "Boston members of the Massachusetts Black Legislative Caucus stand united in opposition to any proposal which calls for an appointed School Committee in the city of Boston" (*Boston Globe*, Mar. 26, 1991, p. 30). Caucus members also indicated their willingness to "block Bolling's proposal unless it was altered to include school reform provisions that [would] give Black, Hispanic and Asian parents a greater voice in management of the schools" (*Boston Globe*, Mar. 26, 1991, p. 30). This was the same measure that contributed to the proposal's defeat in 1990. All five Black legislators attended the news conference.

There was no action until April 1991, when the Black Political Task Force held a public hearing at the Twelfth Street Baptist Church in Roxbury. The hearing was attended by sixty people. Those testifying included Representative Mark Roosevelt and Flynn's political aide Theodore Landsmark, a Black city administrator; each was in favor of an all-appointed board. Representative Nelson Merced and City Councillor Charles Yancey were in favor of an all-elected school committee, and Bruce Bolling advocated for a half-elected, half-appointed panel. The next day, the City Council voted 9 to 4 in favor of a home-rule petition that would replace the thirteen-member elected school committee with a seven-member board appointed by the mayor. The measure was opposed by Yancey and Bolling. The fight for Boston's School Committee now moved again to the state legislative level.

Three steps now remained in the process to abolish the elected school committee: Senate approval, House approval, and the governor's signature. The Black Legislative Caucus led the fight to defeat the proposal in the Senate. First, it held a press conference on the steps of the state House the day the Senate began deliberations on the measure. The conference was attended by parents, ministers, and elected officials who opposed the measure.

Two days later the Senate defeat was orchestrated by Senator Bill Owens and the Black Political Task Force. The task force had suggested that the issue of congressional redistricting be linked with the School Committee question. A meeting was held with state Republican chairman Leon Lombardi on this matter. Republicans, including Governor William Weld, were in favor of redistricting because they wanted to create suburban districts that were not dominated by Boston's democratic voters. The Black legislative delegation also favored redistricting because they believed that making Boston a single district would provide the opportunity to elect a minority representative to Congress. Republican officials took the proposal of the Black Political Task Force to Lt. Governor Paul Cellucci who contacted other Republicans such as Senate party leader David Locke. When the vote was taken, the Republicans joined Owens in voting against the measure. This was a major victory for the Black legislative delegation and the Black Political Task Force.

When the Vault got wind of the Senate vote, it was not pleased. Vault leaders met privately with Mayor Flynn to plan a strategy for the second Senate vote, and they agreed to lobby Senate republicans on the issue. Both the Black legislative delegation and the Vault lobbied hard in the Senate, stalling the vote (*Boston Globe*, May 18, 1991, p. 30; May 23, 1991, p. 42). Lobbying by the business community, however, was not the only factor that determined the final outcome in this case. Two events happened that also influenced the Senate vote.

The *Bay State Banner*, the city's only African American weekly newspaper, published an editorial and political cartoon in support of abolishing the elected school committee. The editorial stated, "Some political activists in the Black community have campaigned against the appointed school committee on the grounds that it would reduce the number of Black elected officials. And indeed it would, but if the Black elected officials have not been able to do the job for their constituents, why should the constituents be concerned about keeping them in office?" The *Bay State Banner's* editorial received major play in the mainstream media, and it was later used by both Senate and House members as the rationale for voting for the appointed board (*Bay State Banner*, May 23, 1991, editorial).

The Interfaith Ministerial Alliance of Greater Boston, an organization of Black clergy, voted to hold a press conference in support of abolishing the elected school committee. It sent a letter to all forty of the state's senators urging them to vote for an appointed school committee. The alliance represented twenty churches with a total of 20,000 members. Their position was in direct opposition to the city's minority state lawmakers. Boston's Black elected officials stated that the alliance did not consult any of them before their vote, but the alliance maintained that they had spent three months discussing the school committee with all sides. The Interfaith Alliance held its press conference on the steps of the state House the same day the Senate voted to abolish the elected school committee.

Senator Bill Owens fought hard to sway the vote with a last minute passionate plea that lasted an hour. Senator Thomas Birmingham, who sponsored the proposal to abolish the school committee, attributed the vote importantly to the actions of the *Bay State Banner* and the ministers. "There has been a suggestion that the Black community was monolithically opposed to the petition," he said. "I think the intervention of leaders—the *Bay State Banner* and the ministers—belied that" (*Boston Globe*, May 29, 1991, p. 1). However, Senator Bill Owens credited the defeat to aggressive lobbying of Senate Republicans by the Vault and business leaders. "The significant factor," Owens said, "was that the Vault got into it" (*Boston Globe*, May 29, 1991, p. 1).

Just before the final Senate vote, the Black Political Task Force and the Black legislative delegation met to discuss further strategies. Fifty Black leaders attended this meeting. Four options were discussed: (1) to delay the vote further by Senator Owens attempting to offer a new amendment; (2) to propose that the Boston Finance Committee be given oversight power over an elected board; (3) to propose that

Mayor Flynn become automatic chair of an elected school committee with the power to cast the final vote in the event of a tie; and (4) to initiate an act of civil disobedience. While the Black leaders were meeting with Senator Owens, an organization called Hispanic and Asian-Americans for Education Reform endorsed the appointed board, creating further division in the minority community.

Mel King led a protest against the appointed board, but the Inter-faith Ministerial Alliance attended as an opposing voice. All of this division within the minority community was covered in the local media. The final Senate vote was 22 to 13 in favor of abolishing the thirteen-member elected school committee; in the House, the vote was 95 to 52 in favor of doing so.

Now it was up to Governor Weld. The city's Black leaders made two attempts to dissuade the governor before he announced his final decision. The Black Political Task Force met with Weld's chief secretary to implore Weld to seek a compromise version of the bill before signing it. Before that, the Black Legislative Caucus had met with Governor Weld urging him to veto the bill. These efforts only succeeded in delaying the inevitable. In July 1991, Governor Weld signed the bill into law that abolished the elected school committee and replaced it with a committee to be appointed by the mayor.

CASE ANALYSIS

The issue of an elected versus an appointed School Committee in Boston was a heavily contested one that lasted for three years. It began formally, with recommendations from the mayor's Special Advisory Committee on School Reform in 1988, and ended in 1991 when the governor signed a law replacing Boston's elected School Committee with a school board the mayor would appoint.

In analyzing this case, we will begin by keeping our promise to cite the importance of certain participants in this event, apart from those we consider the main protagonists. In that connection, we will briefly discuss the roles played by the city and state legislatures and by the elected school committee itself. Following this, we will examine how the case's outcome was shaped by those we call the principal protagonists, namely, Boston's business community, its mayor, and the city's African American leadership.

Obviously, the legislative bodies involved in the case (i.e., Boston's City Council and the Massachusetts state legislature) were fundamental to its legal resolution. Important, too, was the behavior of the elected school committee (a quasi-legislative body itself); otherwise there might not have been a movement to replace it. But in considering the roles of these actors, we are struck by the ultimate power of business interests to influence their behavior or, in the instance of the School Committee, to have it replaced.

One recalls, for example, that Bruce Bolling was stunned by the intensity of Mayor Flynn's lobbying effort on behalf of a referendum that eliminated the half-elected, half-appointed option before the City Council. This option had apparently gained wide community consensus, but the business community was opposed to it. Bolling attributed the intensity of the mayor's pressures directly to the business community.

We also learned that Vault leaders helped persuade state Senate Republicans to rescind their opposition to an appointed-board proposal that was before the Senate. Their opposition had been based upon a bargain made with the Black Political Task Force and the Black legislative delegation.

The influence of business elites over legislatures and elected officials such as mayors is not a new phenomenon. Robert Dahl's classic, *Who Governs?* (1961), is an excellent source for appreciating the power of business oligarchies in municipal settings. But it is instructive to note the role they now play in urban school reform, particularly in the legislative domain.

A recent book by Dan Lewis and Kathryn Nakagawa (1995) sheds important light on this topic. While tracing school decentralization in five major urban cities, Lewis and Nakagawa also depict how elected and business elites generally collaborate to produce mutually acceptable school reform legislation. This legislation, the authors note, tends to focus on governance and consistently precludes the additional funding that inner-city school districts need to gain equity with their suburban counterparts. The authors cite and discuss decentralization in Chicago as the most cogent example of this trend.

While business elites may indeed influence legislative outcomes, the case before us also illustrates an important difference between them and most elected officials. The former can take uncompromising positions, as they did in this instance, while the latter must be ever mindful of voter sentiments and the advantages of political bargaining. This is because elected officials, as career politicians, must seek re-election. They must also be willing to enhance their political positions through agreements with others. These are standard political axioms that have been carefully examined by such scholars as Dahl (1961), Banfield (1961), and Peterson (1976).

One notes, for example, that Mayor Flynn wanted to abandon the fight for an appointed school board when his referendum to create one did not obtain a clear voter mandate. The agreement cited above between upstate Republicans and Black political leaders is an excellent example of how bargaining works in political markets. But for elitist rule to prevail, the main actors in those markets must be controlled. Flynn had to be persuaded to resume his fight for the appointed board; upstate Republicans had to be pressured into changing their votes. In both cases, however, democratic structures and conventional political strategies gave the underdogs (i.e., those with far less power and influence) their best chance of winning—and they almost did.

As for the elected School Committee, one quickly recognizes the role it played in its own demise. The long, politically incestuous relationship with the school bureaucracy, the constant badgering of its superintendents, the failure to attend to important policy issues like student assignment all contributed to a glaring image of ineffectiveness that almost everybody wanted to see changed. It would be useful, however, to briefly examine some of the changes being demanded.

Perhaps the most persistent demand was that the School Committee stop meddling in the administration of the school system and adhere to its policymaking role. As far as we could determine, however, none of the case's protagonists attempted to define what that role actually was. In point of fact, as policymakers, the elected School Committee acted in the same manner as most other school committees and some corporate boards. They functioned as what Kerr (1964) some time ago labeled an "agency of legitimation." Instead of creating policy themselves, such agencies habitually defer that responsibility to their chief executive, then routinely ratify this person's policy initiatives.

This is precisely what happened in the case of superintendent Laval Wilson's Boston Education Plan. Wilson's task forces and the ensuing strategic plan developed from their reports were not created at the

School Committee's suggestion, but at his own. Nor had the committee set educational priorities or a sense of policy direction for Wilson to follow. When the plan was presented, the School Committee ratified it with a minimum of discussion, although the document had far-reaching policy implications, an example being the student assignment issue that the committee was unprepared to address. The procedures followed by the Boston School Committee in this case reflect how boards of directors can often become overdependent on their chief executives. But as policymakers per se, the School Committee's behavior was much more normative than its critics were willing to acknowledge. Also unacknowledged was the fact that school committees sometimes have honest difficulties in determining where policymaking ends and school administration begins. In extreme cases, crossing this imaginary line is easy enough to recognize. However, there are gray areas, as well, and Boston's elected School Committee struggled at length with them at times. One example occurred in 1984 when committee treasurer Dan Burke brought a plan before his colleagues for saving money on the purchase of vehicles used by School Department executives (Edwards 1989). Burke's plan called for purchasing fewer new vehicles by reassigning the use of current ones, and he had worked out a system for how this could be done.

However, some School Committee members felt the assignment of vehicles was an administrative responsibility of the superintendent and that Burke's plan exceeded his policymaking mandate. This particular issue was debated for substantial portions of several public meetings, and Burke's proposal was eventually withdrawn. To many, this was another example of how the School Committee so often wasted its time. In fact, however, the dispute evolved into a serious attempt at role definition, an issue that school committees often fail to address.

For the elected School Committee, however, honest confusion and its conventional, albeit irresponsible, style of policymaking evoked little sympathy from its critics. Instead, the committee had gained such notoriety through its conspicuous failures and tasteless public displays that even its staunchest allies became willing to settle for a partially appointed school board.

As noted, the city's business community was unyielding on this point. We have already substantially alluded to this community's role in the case, and will briefly comment further here.

Having committed itself to helping the public schools, Boston's business leadership was guided by the one principle that best describes its operating style, namely, efficiency. It was in deference to efficiency, we believe, that it focused so sharply on the school system's hierarchical structure. Doing so reflected a traditional top-down business approach, one that a dysfunctional school committee strongly invited. Moreover, while the School Committee stood at the top of its system's hierarchy, it was the mayor who headed the overall municipal superstructure.

Therefore, it was the mayor, business leaders came to believe, who should be held responsible for the schools. They felt that to carry out this responsibility the mayor ought to be authorized to appoint the School Committee. The School Committee, being accountable to the mayor, would then hold the system's professionals accountable through the superintendent of schools. In this manner, accountability would drive the entire system and, ultimately, root out inefficiency in the school bureaucracy.

While this description is, perhaps, a caricature of the management approach Boston's business leaders preferred in this case, we believe it captures the spirit and essential elements of that process. Efficiency, when too vigorously applied, can be hierarchical, impersonal, and punitive. It holds people "accountable" and fires them when they fail; it emphasizes structure, chain of command, and tight control—in short, it becomes McGregor's Theory X (McGregor 1960), updated for age-of-technology consumption. Theory X holds that employees naturally seek to avoid work and must, therefore, be strictly supervised at all times. While a "hard" version of Theory X was not being openly proposed in this case, it was clear that business leaders and many others in the city felt it was "time to get tough" with the Boston School Committee.

This attitude, however, did not preclude the advocacy, at times, of "softer," more potentially productive management approaches by business activists. Their strong support of school-based management (SBM), for example, showed a willingness to experiment with "softer" models based upon Japanese management approaches like Ouchi's Theory Z (1981) and Deming's Total Quality Management (TQM) (1988). These models, which had been adopted by American companies like Ford, IBM, and Polaroid, emphasized shared decision-making, mutual trust, and subtle organizational structures.

Boston's business leaders did not go so far as to propose a TQM model for the school system, but even their advocacy of site-based management revealed certain inconsistencies between such models and the traditional approaches those leaders still basically followed. Under SBM, for example, elected site councils comprised of teachers, parents, community persons, and principals decide how each school is governed. Under an accountability model, however, principals alone are held responsible for their schools. SBM, then, creates a potentially unfair situation for them: they would be held accountable for their schools without having total authority to lead them.

Another inconsistency derives from the following analogy that might be drawn between support of SBM and insistence upon an all-appointed school committee: if democratic governance is valid for individual schools, why should it not be for the system as a whole? Local councils, too, are potentially dysfunctional, as observers of Chicago's and New York City's school governance arrangements can attest to.

In any event, the business community was clearly committed, in this case, to organizational efficiency more than democratic structures. One is struck, in fact, by the strength of their consensus for an appointed school committee; they were unwavering and totally uncompromising on the issue. In addition, of course, they had the resources to achieve their goal.

These included decisive influence over the state legislature, the City Council, and the mayor. They also had a paid, permanent public relations arm in BMRB and an unpaid one in the Boston media, which rather consistently supported their positions. Media coverage also often coincided with initiatives on behalf of the appointed board. In addition, the business community created a modest, for them, "war chest," which was funneled to the mayor through his Better Education Committee. To our knowledge, their opponents in the Black community had no "war chest" at all. Indeed, except for an early *Globe* editorial in support of the elected board (a position that was quickly reversed), business leadership seemed indifferent to Black political interests in this case. For them, the only important issue appeared to be efficient management of the Boston public schools.

The mayor, in our view, was no more than the principal agent through whom the business community's agenda was acted upon. It was, no doubt, true that the mayor preferred to have control over the city's public schools, but we doubt that he would have pursued that goal without the business community's support. We certainly do not believe he would have done so over its strong objections. In the end, business communities have the power to threaten the economic well-being of cities and, at some level, mayors must always be aware of this reality.

In his pursuit of an appointed board, Flynn's foremost strategy was a standard one—divide and conquer. This strategy was directed mainly at the African American community since it presented the most formidable, persistent opposition to his goal.

Notwithstanding the mayor's ties to certain clergy and others in the Black community, there was understandable community ambivalence toward the elected School Committee. Most of its residents were reluctant to lose their vote and the type of representation that an elected school board provided. On the other hand, the community was unanimous in its desire for better schools. For this important reason, some residents felt that the fundamental issues in this case were educational, rather than political. Others were convinced that its political importance should take precedence.

From the outset, Mayor Flynn tapped into and exploited this dilemma. He strongly emphasized the educational needs of the schools and laid the blame for their problems squarely at the feet of the elected School Committee. He could point with evidence and conviction at the School Committee's continuing failures and, at the same time, all but ignore the issue of Black political empowerment. After all, he had first been challenged for election to his position by an African American candidate, Mel King, who showed surprising political strength early in the campaign. Therefore, the loss of elected representation from a community whose political growth was noticeably on the rise was not likely to disturb him.

Flynn's strategy of dividing the Black community coincided with the decision to strengthen his campaign by creating blue-ribbon commissions that would "study" the governance issue. In addition to appointing African Americans to those panels, he selected a Black person of status to head each of them. This is a "textbook" strategy cited, for example, by Peterson (1981) in his study of how post–civil rights municipal governments deflect equity, or redistribution, demands of a community's disadvantaged segments. One counter-redistribution tactic identified by Peterson is "the identification of group leaders and giving them special concessions. . . . [They] can be employed in relevant public-service positions, [or be] given an honored position in policy deliberations" (1981:180). This strategy is called co-optation and appears to be precisely the one employed in this case. Each of the commissions appointed by Mayor Flynn recommended exactly as he wished on the question of school governance, while the other areas they were charged to consider went largely ignored.

While co-optation of this sort seems rather transparent, it is not so easy to prevent. For one thing, citizens of stature in a community are responsible individuals who usually feel it their duty to assist in a municipal crisis. For another, the mayor can appoint persons on both sides of an issue to such panels while ensuring that those who favor his own position are in the majority. Our interviews with commission members indicate that this did, in fact, occur. Certain members of Flynn's Special Commission on Public Education, for example, strongly preferred a partially elected School Committee but were in the minority on the panel. The commission's official recommendations represented the majority view, while positions of minority dissent received virtually no attention.

A further variant of the "divide and conquer" strategy may be seen in the appointments Flynn made to his Better Education Committee. In this case, committee membership was ethnically integrated and confined to those who supported the appointed school board. One advantage of carefully integrating this body was that it could be pointed to—and was—as proof that Black support of an elected school committee was far from unanimous.

In our opinion, establishing cross-ethnic commissions and a support group of the kind just cited were the most effective actions taken by Mayor Flynn in behalf of his cause. His other efforts, such as lobbying the City Council and state legislature, seemed more pro forma to us and, in any case, were being carried out, perhaps more effectively, by members of those bodies themselves.

When examining the role that African American leadership played in this case, one is struck, at first, by how divided that leadership seemed to be. As previously noted, there was an understandable dilemma among African Americans that would partially explain this. Most felt their political interests would be best served through an elected school committee, but opponents of the elected committee and the committee's behavior itself raised doubts about its ability to serve Black educational interests.

Notice that embedded in this controversy was the unexamined assumption that school governance and student achievement were so critically linked that governance should become the main focus for improving Boston's schools. This point of departure had been decided upon by ruling elites, and its implicit assumption was never subject to serious debate. There might have been other priorities for improving a school system like Boston's, however. Equitable funding for its public schools, the recruitment of talented teachers, and the creation of schools that are supportive learning environments are three options that come to mind, but governance became the principal issue the public was constrained to consider in this case. This posed a serious dilemma for some African Americans.

Nevertheless, if the mayor's School Committee referendum was an important measure—and it is certainly the best empirical data we have on the matter—then the Black community was not nearly as divided as the appointed board's proponents would have had the public believe. On the contrary, the overwhelming majority of voters in the Black community, and in working-class White ones as well, preferred an elected school committee. Even when this option no longer seemed feasible, a broad consensus developed across the city for, at least, a partially elected school board. Critical to that consensus were the roles played by Black elected officials, each of whom supported some form of elected representation on the School Committee.

To be sure, unanimity did not exist among Blacks on this issue, but any impression of deep, widespread division among them can be best attributed, we believe, to the media exposure provided for strategically timed statements and demonstrations by certain clergy and other conservative elements in the Black community. Indeed, many members of the media themselves supported an appointed School Committee, including the *Boston Globe* and the *Bay State Banner*, an African American weekly with a more or less traditional editorial policy.

One wonders, in fact, about the true leadership status and strengths of the Black clergy who supported an appointed school committee while African American voters in the same communities where their churches are located emphatically rejected it. This suggests, perhaps, that clergy leadership authority in spiritual matters does not automatically extend into the political domain without advice and consent from a larger representation of the community.

What most often appeared to be division among Black leaders, in fact, were differences over process rather than differences over principles. In principle, Black leadership seemed strongly in favor of elected representation of some kind on the School Committee. Blacks, in general, were politically flexible in this case, as were most Whites, including the mayor. It was mainly business interest groups that were inflexible. Their inflexibility defeated a community spirit of compromise on this issue.

To the extent, therefore, that a search for compromise implied division, then this form of division was one of the challenges Black leadership had to face. To better identify the range of these challenges, we have divided them into two general categories: vertical challenges and horizontal ones. Vertical challenges involved efforts to strengthen support for the elected school committee beyond the Black community; horizontal efforts were aimed at gaining support within the community. Success in this case required that both categories be addressed at once. This conceptual framework is adapted from African American sociologist James Blackwell, who noted that, "two kinds of forces have always been at work in the Black community: (1) centripetal forces—elements that draw members of a minority group toward their own group, and (2) centrifugal forces—those elements that magnetize members in the direction of the dominant group" (1975:282).

To analyze specific vertical and horizontal actions by Black leadership in this case, we have selected bargaining models employed by Peterson (1976) in his study of Chicago's school politics immediately following the civil rights era. Peterson identifies two forms of bargaining that are useful for our purposes: pluralist and ideological.

Pluralist bargaining attempts to maximize mutual political advantage through compromise. Political majorities are attained in this manner when no one political group has the votes to gain victory alone. Under these circumstances, coalitions are formed, and pledges of mutual support are exchanged. In the case before us, the agreement between upstate Senate Republicans and the Black Political Task Force is a good example of pluralist bargaining. When examining Black leadership's vertical efforts, the pluralist model is especially applicable.

Ideological bargaining, by contrast, tends to reject compromise. Ideologues act out of philosophical conviction and deeply held principles. This form of bargaining is often confrontational and generally produces winners and losers. In the case before us, the business community behaved in an ideological fashion.

When examining Black leadership's efforts in this matter, one is immediately impressed by one conspicuous failure and another notable success. The failure was the inability of African American leaders and the appointed board's opponents in working-class White communities to forge an alliance. Indeed, we found no serious efforts to do so on either side. We attribute this failure to the dominance of ideological attitudes, when pluralist behavior seemed clearly indicated.

Another example was the formation of Senator Bill Owens's Right to Vote group. This was an all-Black organization created to help save the elected school committee. White membership in this group might have importantly increased its strength but was rejected out of ideological conviction. Both examples, in our opinion, illustrate the deep and enduring nature of the racial hostility that Boston's desegregation struggle unleashed. Because that hostility is sustained by racism's seemingly permanent social presence, Black pluralism is under constant ideological challenge.

For this reason, the bargain with upstate Senate Republicans, initiated by the Black Political Task Force and the Black legislative delegation, was all the more remarkable. To even attempt such a bargain reflected a gifted political imagination. To us, failure to achieve the ultimate goal of saving the elected committee was not so important as the "lesson of a good example" this effort provided. In our opinion, this was Black leadership's most notable pluralist achievement in the case.

Elsewhere, one is struck by the extent of Black racial isolation on elected pluralist bodies, such as the Boston School Committee, the City Council, and state legislature. On the School Committee, for example, its four Black members were joined by only one White in opposing the firing in 1990 of Laval Wilson, Boston's first African American superintendent of schools. One also notes the isolation of the City Council's two African American members, Charles Yancey and Bruce Bolling. Even Bolling, who initially seemed especially willing to cooperate with Mayor Flynn in this matter, wound up with

Yancey as the lone dissenters at times on City Council resolutions. In the state Senate, Bill Owens was its only Black member, and he made the lone final plea to that body in an effort to save the elected School Committee.

Racial isolation of this kind encourages Black ideological bonding and a disinclination among African Americans to forge pluralist alliances. Yet, without such alliances Black political strength will not develop because African Americans alone do not comprise a political majority. Thus, both ideological solidarity and pluralist coalitions are essential for them.

We would like to conclude, by briefly discussing a final factor we deem indispensable to Black solidarity, namely, open and honest internal communication. Communication of this kind is necessary, not only to share information, but to generate ideas and strategies, air differences, and ensure the active participation of all community elements.

The one outstanding effort in this case was the regular Thursday morning meetings at Bob the Chef's restaurant convened by Mel King. Broad community representation was present at those meetings, and from what we have gathered, the dialogue was open and quite honest. Because of the rapidly changing pace of events in the case, however, the meetings were inadequate to meet the communication needs of the wider Black community.

One consequence was a communications gap that was, perhaps, best illustrated by a somewhat surprising proposal made by African American state representative Nelson Merced. Merced, who favored an elected school committee, insisted that parental empowerment be linked to the school committee issue. He introduced this recommendation during state legislative negotiations, apparently without consultation with the local Black leadership that had spearheaded the school committee fight. Not only was Merced's recommendation uncoordinated with their efforts, but it lost support for the compromise proposal of a part-appointed, and part-elected committee that teacher groups and other sources were ready to give. The Merced parent-empowerment proposal caused the compromised proposal to fail in the Senate.

This suggests a feature of African American leadership structure that remains largely unaddressed, namely, what Dahl calls "petty sovereignties" (1961:184 ch.15). Under this informal leadership structure, particular issue areas are controlled by different sets of community leaders. As long as leadership activity in one area does not conflict with that in others, "sovereigns" go about their business without much communication with one another. This appears to be the case in Boston's African American community, where different individuals seem to have leadership status in such areas as housing, education, community development, and politics. Merced, perhaps, was simply not in the habit of communicating regularly with local Black education leaders and those who, in this case, were working in their behalf.

In reviewing this case, we remain deeply concerned about some of the issues it has illuminated. We remain concerned, for example, about the education of Black children, whose immediate school needs were marginal to this debate. Where Black leadership is concerned, we hope that losing the elected school committee will not drive it further away from the schools. In our opinion, this leadership was not attending sufficiently to the schools in the first place. Education, for it, had become very much a Black "sovereignty" area, but, frankly, the educational "sovereigns" were not ruling well. Nor should public schools be the exclusive "turf" of any single community interest.

Where the business community and mayor are concerned, we hope that they will now focus more consistently on the educational needs of the schools. Indeed, there has been a recent infusion of foundation money into the school system that has been aimed in this direction, but both the mayor and the business community are mistaken if they believe that transforming schools is mainly a question of efficiency. School improvement, at bottom, is relational; it involves the ability to reach and understand both the human and academic potential of children. It must also be continually aware of their families and the social contexts of learning.

In that connection, the city's power elite are also mistaken if they believe racism in education will disappear through the "efficient management" of schools. In fact, preoccupation with efficiency often can become a tool for denying racism's destructive role in the lives of minority students and their families. The city's elites, therefore, must devote far more focused attention than they presently do to issues of race and social class. Unless they are willing to do so, the social peace and economic prosperity Boston is now so proud of will have an unpredictable and in all likelihood, unstable duration.

From this case study we have learned many things. However, three ideas—diversity, flexibility, and legitimatization—stand out. This case revealed that diversified decision-making structures are beneficial for all groups, including dominant and subdominant people of power. Failure is a likely outcome when the number of people who are privy to a discussion of alternative public policies is so small that it lacks access to the range of possible responses by the community at large, and, therefore, makes inappropriate assumptions regarding the liabilities and assets of various proposals.

Also, this case reveals that flexibility is essential in achieving negotiated solutions to complex community issues. Although the proposal for an appointed school committee advocated by business leaders in Boston prevailed, it almost failed because of their inflexible stance. The less powerful minority and working-class interest groups almost won as they modified their initial position in favor of an elected school committee only to embrace a part-elected, part-appointed group. Such flexibility is something of value in bringing together disparate interest groups in the community. The inflexibility of business interests opposed the compromise and probably would have resulted in failure of the appointed school committee proposal, if Representative Merced had not committed the error of inserting the parent empowerment clause into the pending compromise bill for a part-elected, part-appointed school committee.

Finally, we learned that proposals for community action should be legitimized by groups that have the capacity to determine what is in the public interest. Dominant people of power have formal and standing decision-making groups to which they may turn to legitimize their proposals. These legitimizing groups usually are controlled by the dominants, indeed, in the case of BMRB, created by them. Such groups as the Chamber of Commerce, the Municipal Research Bureau, the City Council, and the Board of Education perform these functions. Subdominant people of power have few groups to which they can turn for legitimization and usually must create a new such structure to assess new and emerging issues and to determine whether their implementation is in the public interest. When legitimization structures are not used by dominant or subdominant groups, the possibility exists that some policy advocates may mistake their private interests for the public interests and propose actions that benefit some of the people but not all of the people.

REFERENCES

Banfield, E. 1961. *Political Influence.* New York: The Free Press.
Bay State Banner. 1991. "Editorial." May 23.
Blackwell, James. 1975. *The Black Community.* New York: Dodd, Mead and Co.
Blackwell, James and P. Hart. 1982. *Cities, Suburbs and Blacks.* Dix Hills, NY: General Hall.
Bolling, Bruce. 1993. Boston City Councillor. Personal Interview. October 26, at City Hall.
Boston Globe. 1989. "Black Group Cool to Flynn Plan." August 16, p. 33.
Boston Globe. 1989. "Flynn Creates Group to Push for Appointed School Board." September 12, p. 26.
Boston Globe. 1989. "Council May Add Options to Flynn School Proposal." September 20, p. 35.
Boston Globe. 1989. "No on Question Two." November 1, p. 18.
Boston Globe. 1989. "Now Flynn Aides Push School Board Proposal." November 4, p. 26.
Boston Globe. 1989. "Flynn's School Plan Gains Razor Thin Win." November 8, p. 1.
Boston Globe. 1989. "Firm Gives $150,000 to Change School Panel." December 8, p. 42.
Boston Globe. 1989. "Flynn Turns to Parents for Ideas on School Panel." December 30, p. 21.
Boston Globe. 1990. "Two Plans Offered to Alter School Committee." August 16, p. 36.
Boston Globe. 1990. "Movement on School Change." September 5, p. 21.
Boston Globe, 1990. "School Overhaul Plan Supported at Hearing." September, p. 19.
Boston Globe. 1990c. "Analyst Says Combined Board Is Wrong Answer." September 10, p. 17.
Boston Globe. 1990d. "An Accountable School Board." September 10, p. 14.
Boston Globe. 1991a. "Legislature Rejects Flynn's School Board Plan, Offers a New One." March 26, p. 30.
Boston Globe. 1991b. "Black Law Makers Assail Plan for Appointed School Committee." March 27, p. 26.
Boston Globe. 1991c. "GOP Helps Stall Bill to Revise School Panel." May 18, p. 30.
Boston Globe. 1991d. "Door of Vault Opens to Lobby." May 23, p. 42.

Boston Globe. 1991e. "Senate Boasts Effort to Eliminate the City's Elected School Board." May 29, p. 1.

Dahl, R. 1961. *Who Governs?* New Haven, CT: Yale University Press.

Deming, W. E. 1988. *Out of Crisis*. Cambridge, MA: MIT Press.

Edwards, R. 1989. *How Boston Selected Its First Black Superintendent of Schools*. Unpublished doctoral dissertation, Harvard Graduate School of Education, Cambridge, MA.

Kerr, N.D. 1964. "The School Board as an Agency of Legitimation." *Sociology of Education*. (Autumn), 1964.

Lewis, D. and K. Nakagawa. 1995. *Race and Educational Reform in the American Metropolis: A Study of School Desegregation*. Albany, NY: State University of New York Press.

Lucas, J. Anthony. 1985. *Common Ground*. New York: Alfred A. Knopf.

McGregor, D. 1960. *The Human Side of Enterprise*. New York: McGraw-Hill.

Murningham, M. 1984. *Getting Power Back: Court Restoration of Executive Authority in Boston City Government*. Boston: Institute of Public Affairs, University of Massachusetts.

Ouchi, W. G. 1981. *Theory Z*. Reading, MA: Addison-Wesley.

Peterson, P. 1981. *City Limits*. Chicago: University of Chicago Press.

Peterson, P. 1976. *Politics Chicago Style*. Chicago: University of Chicago Press.

Ross, J. M. and M. Berg. 1981. *I Respectfully Disagree with the Judge's Order*. Washington, DC: University Press of America.

Schrag, P. 1967. *Village School Downtown*. Boston: Beacon Press.

Tyler, Sam. Director, Boston Municipal Research Bureau. Personal Interview, November 16, 1993.

Yancey, Charles. Boston City Councillor, Personal Interview, November 22, 1993 at City Hall.

4. ____ Conclusion: Making Alliances and Building Coalitions

A generation ago, Robert Dahl studied public education in New Haven, Connecticut, and found some characteristics of the school system there that we find similar to those emerging in Boston today. For example, Dahl found that the chief center of direct influence on public education was the mayor and his appointees on the Board of Education, rather than the superintendent (1961:152), and "that some ethnic, religious and professional distributions [in School Board appointments are] assumed to be necessary" (1961:150). "Considering the nature of the task assigned to public schools," Dahl states, "it is hardly surprising that control over the schools is seen as worth fighting for by leaders and many different groups" (1961:143). Because these findings in another New England community correspond with what is happening in Boston, it is possible that our documentation of the Boston experience in public education may be of help to other communities.

Hunter (1953) hypothesizes that local community decision making is greatly influenced by an elite oligarchy that could be described as economic notables (individuals who gain influence from their wealth, high social standing, and economic dominance). However, Dahl believes that there are multiple styles of leadership in local communities, including "executive-centered coalitions" and "independent sovereignties with spheres of influence" (Dahl 1961:184). In New Haven, Dahl discovered that these coalitions "are coordinated largely by elected leaders who draw on special skills and resources of influence that leaders without public office are not likely to have" (1961:186). This, in part, is true of Boston. However, our research discovered that the coalitions among dominant people of power tend to be coordinated by the paid executives of business special interest groups, such as the Municipal Research Bureau and the Private Industry Council. Executives of these groups seem to have more coordinating influence than some public office holders, although elected officials by reason of their position are very important in community decision making.

The subdominant people of power in Boston tend to be organized into independent sovereignties with spheres of influence. Dahl describes this leadership arrangement as one in which "each issue-area is controlled by a different set of top leaders." These sovereigns, according to Dahl, "go about their business without much communication or negotiation" (1961:188).

Boston's Black political leaders are involved in each of the educational issues presented in this book. However, the participation of Blacks who were not public officials tended to be issue-specific. In the appointed school committee issue the Black leaders, other than those affiliated with government, tended to be different from those who participated in the hiring and firing of the first Black superintendent. While there is some overlap in Black leadership and organizations involved in the two educational issues discussed, the number that participated in one but not the other issue is sufficiently different to declare that leadership in the Boston Black community is issue-specific, at least in the area of education.

To overcome the liabilities of the "Territorial Imperative" syndrome discussed by Robert Ardrey and seen in the Boston Black community, the negotiating process must be humanized with open communication so that public interest and personal concern can be mediated (Ardrey 1966:79), and so the leaders in one special area may see how their strategies complement those of leaders in another area. Failure to do this could result in arbitrary and capricious actions that may benefit one personally but is harmful to group interests.

The reconciliation of individual and group interests as well as the interests of a plurality of groups is necessary, even essential, in human societies. The Boston Black community is found wanting in the development of social structures to do this. In only one of the educational issues was there an attempt to negotiate in a continuous way a consensus around the valid but different opinions that existed within the Black community. Concerning the appointed versus elected school committee issue, Mel King, a former candidate for the office of mayor in Boston, assembled representatives of the diverse interest groups in the Black community for regular meetings at Bob the Chef's restaurant. This consensus-building operation lasted a few weeks and then ended. After the disintegration of this consultation process, Black leaders were left to negotiate with their opposites without a coherent philosophy and without a series of community-defined goals regarding what should be accomplished in behalf of subdominants in the community.

There is evidence the home-rule petition that was filed with the state for a local school committee that would be part-elected and part-appointed, which was endorsed by several Black associations, would have passed if a Black state representative had not attached to the proposal an amendment to create school councils that would have the power to hire and fire principals. This amendment frightened the teachers union that in turn marshaled its power to influence the state Senate to reject the proposal, after the House of Representatives had approved it. Without evaluating the merits of the amendment, it is safe to say that the goal the amendment sought to achieve was secondary or even tertiary to the goal of the major proposal supported by most people in the Black community to create a school committee half-elected and half-appointed. Failure of the Black community to achieve this goal was due largely to the absence of consensus-building and coordinating structures among the people.

Regarding the hiring of the first Black superintendent in Boston, Black leaders on the Search Committee acknowledged that they represented different constituencies among people of color and did not attempt to act as a unified group. Consequently, Blacks on the Search Committee did not maintain constant communication with one another so that their diverse strategies could be coordinated into complementary actions. While failure to coordinate their actions did not jeopardize the hiring of the first Black school superintendent in Boston (largely because White business leaders also supported the Black candidate), such uncoordinated activity could have been harmful if White business interests had withdrawn their support. Thus, the appointment of the first Black superintendent in Boston was due, in part, to the coalition that Blacks established with White business leaders, conservative Whites on the School Committee, and with a

Latino member on the School Committee. Without these linkages, Black votes alone were insufficient to elect Laval Wilson.

Some variant of a regular mass meeting that was effective in Montgomery, Alabama, during the successful bus boycott might be an effective communication and coordination model that could be used in Boston and elsewhere in the nation among subdominant people of power. During the brief time that such an approach was used in Boston at the gatherings at the restaurant, it proved effective. Unity is something of value in community organization. It should be realized, however, that unity cannot be ordered but must be achieved by way of communication, coordination, and negotiation.

Dominant people of power can achieve communication and coordination easier than subdominant people of power and, therefore, have an advantage because they tend to function in a bureaucratic rather than a consensus mode. Moreover, the dominant people of power tend to operate through executive-centered coalitions (Dahl 1961:184). Thus, organizations in bureaucratic coalitions, such as the Boston Municipal Research Bureau or the Private Industry Council, have staff to perform administrative activities such as information dissemination, negotiations, and other functions. The bureaucratic mode of operation of dominant people of power is fundamentally different from the consensus mode of operation found among subdominant people of power. While one kind of mode may appear to be more effective for a specific group, in community decision making, bureaucratic and consensus modes complement each other. In this respect, subdominant people of power do not have to act like dominant people of power to be effective.

In the appointed versus elected school committee issue, the blacks in cooperation with working-class neighborhoods of Irish and Italian voters almost derailed the movement with a large vote just short of a majority of the people who went to the polls. These groups tend to feel that their interests are not adequately considered in public policymaking by citywide representatives and therefore, prefer representatives elected in single-member districts. Black and White working-class people had a common concern. Their joint vote was so large (although less than a majority) that the mayor could not claim a local mandate to petition the state to change the method of selecting School Committee members.

Although the joint voting of Black and White working-class communities initially stalled the movement to change the way the Boston School Committee is selected, neither the Black working class nor the white working class cultivated its racially opposite constituency for the purpose of creating a more enduring alliance. Eventually, the business and political dominants who advocated for an appointed school committee found alternative ways of gaining support for their proposal and outmaneuvered their adversaries. If the working-class Black, Irish, and Italian populations who preferred an elected school committee had deliberately worked together as a coalition, they could have been almost invincible. Because these groups did not establish an alliance and work together as a coalition, ultimately they were defeated.

Realizing the value of coalition building, the political establishment has increasingly reached out to racial and ethnic minority groups to serve as members on its various councils, commissions, and committees. Some might call this "reaching out" cooptation. However, subdominant people of power seem to be entrapped in an ideology of self-sufficiency that seldom includes the building of coalitions and the making of alliances with diverse population groups. Also, it could be that racial minorities do not reach out to other groups because they fear betrayal.

The issue of coalition-building was faced squarely by Martin Luther King, Jr. in 1966 when he and other civil rights leaders decided to continue the solo march that James Meredith had begun in Mississippi. Meredith was wounded by gunshots but not killed on his one-man march to Jackson, Mississippi, to prove that Blacks were no longer afraid of Whites in that state and to encourage Blacks to register and vote (Oates 1982:381). The march was continued in "the spirit of Meredith" by the Congress of Racial Equality (CORE), the Student Nonviolent Coordinating Committee (SNCC), and the Southern Christian Leadership Conference (SCLC) (Oates 1982:382).

The marchers left for Jackson, Mississippi, on Highway 51 from the spot where Meredith was wounded. While marching, King overheard young people affiliated with CORE and SNCC berating and rejecting the idea of nonviolence. Then the issue of White participation in the march came up. The young people and leaders affiliated with CORE and SNCC wanted to bar Whites, saying this was Blacks' march and that Whites were not welcome. After the day's march and during the evening hours, King pleaded with the participants "to remain true to nonviolence." With reference to the inclusion of Whites, King reminded the leaders of the organizations cooperating in the march that "racial understanding came from contact"; thus he insisted that the march should be interracial. Moreover, he felt that to bar Whites from the march would be "a shameful repudiation" of other Whites who "had bled and died on civil rights battlefronts." Despite the grumbling of some Blacks, the march continued under a nonviolent and interracial banner at King's insistence and was successfully completed (Oates 1982:381–83).

King knew that "alliance relationships. . . are the keys to political progress" (King 1967:151). He sincerely believed that "effective political power for [Blacks] cannot come through separatism" (King 1967:48). One should not construe this quotation to mean that King was an absolute assimilationist. It is more appropriate to call him a pragmatist, one whose strategy is derived from the situations in which one finds oneself. While acknowledging that Blacks "need organized strength," he explained that "strength will only be effective when it is consolidated through constructive alliances" (King 1967:50).

The case studies in this book illustrate the validity of King's thinking. Blacks won when Laval Wilson was appointed as the first Black superintendent of the Boston public schools. However, their victory was a combination of their own efforts and the efforts of others with which they were affiliated, such as Latinos, White business leaders, and a politician of Italian ancestry. King knew that "Organized strength of [Blacks] alone would have been insufficient to move Congress and the administration without the weight of the aroused conscience of White America." "In the period ahead," King predicted, "[Blacks] will continue to need this support" (King 1967:51). An examination of Black leadership in public education in Boston confirms King's prediction. King admired the "grassroots" organizing skills of people like Saul Alinsky and believed that self-help local groups were essential. However, according to biographer William Robert Miller, "he did not regard self-help as a panacea but only as one element in a program that would require municipal, state, and above all, comprehensive federal action" (Miller 1968:250).

Community organization specialist Roland Warren informs us that "each of a community's units typically has both vertical and horizontal aspects" and that, sometimes, "vertical ties are stronger than the horizontal ties" (Warren 1963:241, 242). An error committed by many local community organizers is to focus on horizontal ties only. Early on, King realized that strong local organizations are essential in redressing the grievances of oppressed people, but that they are strengthened by vertical ties beyond the local community. Referring to the value of vertical linkages, King said that "an occasional word from [the Office of the President of the United States] counseling the nation on the moral aspects of integration and the need to comply with the law, might have saved the South from much. . . confusion and terror" (King 1958:172).

Blacks in Boston almost won in their effort to prevent an appointed school committee by making an alliance at the state level with the Republican party to implement policies that fulfilled their mutual self-interests. Eventually, the Republican party backed away from its agreement with Boston Blacks because of countervailing pressure from local business interests. While the proposed alliance fell apart before it could benefit Boston Blacks, the negotiations indicated that some individuals in the Boston Black community had a good understanding of the value of extra-community leverage and vertical linkages in solving local social problems.

In a community in which there are distinct leadership styles, such as executive-centered coalitions found largely among dominant people of power who are White and decentralized clusters of leaders largely found among subdominant people of power who are Black, conflict and misunderstandings are inevitable. Effective policies and plans that promote the public interest are likely to be those that are forged on the anvil of controversy by competing special interest groups. It is more appropriate to encounter controversy around the conference table where it can be dealt with in a controlled way, where bargaining, trade-offs, and compromises can be worked out.

For these reasons, decision-making groups ought to be diversified, consisting of dominant and subdominant people of power. Diversity is the source of our salvation and is the proper antidote for fear, suspicion, and misunderstanding. Indeed, when the deliberations of governing bodies become too peaceful, the possibility is that they may have become too homogenous and unrepresentative of the varying interests in urban communities. An analysis of the Black community and its problem-resolving strategies has revealed the benefits of diversity and the value of making alliances and building coalitions.

We have discussed the benefits of coalition building. In the introductory chapters, we promised to answer a few additional questions such as these:

- Is the decision-making structure of the Black community monolithic or polylithic?
- Which institutional system in the community at-large does the Black population have the greatest access to?
- How do Black community leaders coordinate their goals and activities?
- How effective are Black leaders in converting Black concerns into public policy agenda items?
- Do Whites deliberately attempt to divide Black leaders for the purpose of controlling the Black community?
- How does Black community action materialize in the face of widening social class divisions within African American communities?

With reference to the decision-making structure in the Black community in Boston, we find that it is basically polylithic. The case studies indicate that some Black leaders tend to focus on certain issues that interest them, while other Black leaders tend to focus on a different set of issues that interest them. Black political leaders and civil rights organization leaders tend to be involved in all issues. However, Black leaders other than those in politics or civil rights organizations tend to be drawn to specific issues or specific clusters of issues. This pattern, as noted earlier, coincides with Robert Dahl's findings in New Haven. Dahl discovered that community leadership is sometimes divided into "independent sovereignties with spheres of influence" (Dahl 1961:184).

In such cases, according to Dahl, "fighting it out" between sovereignties is avoided when policies advocated are viewed as being "complementary in the sense that a gain for one entails no loss for the other and may even produce a benefit" (1961:188). This finding indicates that conflict-resolution strategies for Blacks and other subdominants are necessary, since "fighting it out" publicly when differences arise would signal disunity and, therefore, would be detrimental to the advancement of the agendas of Blacks. Our findings in Boston indicate that, in general, the Black community leadership structure should be classified as more polylithic and less monolithic.

A polylithic leadership structure of necessity must establish processes of communication and coordination to facilitate cooperation. We promised to examine whether or not such processes are present in the Boston Black community and, if they are, whether or not they are effective. Our conclusion is that few permanent communication processes have been established among Blacks for dealing with educational issues in Boston. The Black Political Task Force had the possibility of serving this function but has never achieved the stability necessary to perform this role. It and other groups have not developed effective conflict-resolution methods that will permit participants to reconcile their differences and move forward in cooperation.

To achieve consensus about community goals, the Black community in Boston has to establish ad hoc communicating and coordinating arrangement for each issue. Sometimes the ad hoc system works; sometimes it fails. In Boston, there was evidence of both success and failure. Even when successful, ad hoc arrangements for communication and coordination tend to terminate prematurely. The absence of a continuous system of communication and coordination is a serious deficiency for the Black community in Boston and its polylithic leadership structure.

While Blacks in Boston have had fairly good experience as leaders in several different institutional systems, such as private education, athletics, religion, business, and medicine, they have achieved greatest visibility in the political sphere. Black political leaders tend to be involved in a wide range of community issues, more so than leaders in other spheres.

Because of the absence of effective communicating and coordinating processes in the Black community, leaders sometimes function very much as if they were "Lone Rangers." More consultation would enhance the effects of their efforts in behalf of the Black community. Rather than following the dictates of their community, Black political leaders often are forced to get out front as public opinion-makers. They must assume this role because there are few organizations other than churches into which they can tap to obtain an informed opinion of what the Black community really wants.

In the case of an appointed versus an elected school committee, Black elected officials, in general, were strongly supportive of their community's rejection of the referendum for an appointed committee. In this connection, Black elected leadership seemed more representative of the community's wishes than several of its religious leaders who, for various reasons, supported the mayor's decision to seek an appointed committee. Again, an effective intragroup conflict-resolution mechanism might have prevented the "in-fighting" by different Black groups.

There is evidence that Whites are beginning to reach out to the Black community in Boston. There are several ways to interpret this. Some Blacks believe that inviting increased numbers of Blacks to serve on official committees, commissions, and councils is a technique to divide and conquer the Black community. Others believe the outreach represents increased maturity by Whites who recognize that their knowledge about community affairs is incomplete and must be complemented with the wisdom of Blacks.

In the case of Dr. Laval Wilson's selection as superintendent of schools, for example, one encounters a deliberate attempt by White leadership—in the person of School Committee president John Nucci—to improve the chances of minority candidates to win the superintendency. Not only did Nucci appoint Blacks to the Search Committee that recommended Wilson to the School Committee, he appointed an African American woman to chair the Search Committee. Nucci also appointed and arranged the Search Committee's membership in a manner that ensured a clearly liberal majority on the panel. In the end, two of the final three candidates selected by the Search Committee were minorities, and Wilson, the African American candidate, was selected as superintendent.

In the case of the appointed versus elected school committee issue, it was evident that the mayor wanted the authority to appoint such a group. Therefore, one has to view his selection of Blacks for the committees he created to "study" this issue as the selection of individuals in sympathy with his goal. In fact, the mayor's behavior in this instance seemed to employ certain counter-redistribution principles outlined by Peterson (1981) and alluded to earlier.

For example, Peterson points out that one form of "cooptation" employed by municipal power structures involves the "identification of group leaders and giving them special concession," which might include "public service positions, an honored position in policy deliberations, or [invitations] to participate in conferences" (1981:180). The appointment of reputable African American community leaders, first to the mayor's Special Advisory Committee on School Reform in 1988, then later to the Special Committee on Public Education in 1989, seems to echo the kinds of strategies Peterson discussed. So, too, would the mayor's creation of the Better Education Committee in 1989 that included minorities among its leadership, and that became the vehicle through which the business community funneled an estimated $150,000 in support of the campaign to create an appointed school board. Politically, it is indispensable for municipal power structures to include minorities in decision-making processes if the power structures hope to avoid minority veto power. This is a fundamental lesson learned during the protest era of the 1960s. Moreover, broadly based policy decisions are generally more workable, since they tend to be better informed when they emerge from heterogeneous groups. Thus, in recent years, most of the advisory groups appointed by officers of government in Boston have been multiracial in composition.

While inclusion has been beneficial for Blacks, it also has had troubling side effects. For example, some Blacks in our study have not yet decided how to react to public policy proposals about which they have serious questions when these proposals are issued by establishment bodies in which other Blacks have participated.

Another matter that requires further study is what Blacks think about local control. In general, they tend to exalt "grassroots" efforts and local control because these are closer to the people. Blacks in Boston and elsewhere in the nation are at times distrustful of bureaucratic systems in which decisions are made distant from the localities in which people live. Yet, the biggest "deal" the Blacks in Boston almost pulled off was a deal with a state political party that would have protected Black local interests pertaining to the election of school committee members. Moreover, in years gone by it was federal government and to a lesser degree state government that protected the civil rights of Blacks more than local governments. In contemporary times, this protection has somewhat diminished. Thus, it is a dilemma regarding who to trust—policymakers nearby or policymakers far away. On this matter Blacks in Boston and elsewhere are in a quandary as to whether to advocate a centralized or decentralized approach in public policymaking especially with reference to education.

Another area we wanted to address, but lacked the data to consider in depth, relates to the implications of Black social class divisions for local community action. These divisions did not appear to have significant impact on either of the cases reported in this study, both of which focused on education. This, therefore, is an issue for further study.

Black support for Laval Wilson, at least initially, was almost unanimous. The strongest early advocacy for his superintendency originated among Black elites, but there was little internal dissent from this position across social class lines. Where dissent did materialize it was over educational policies that would effect Black youth. Some felt Wilson's approach to be too conservative, too inflexible, but this criticism did not appear to be class-based.

There was general support, both among Black citizens and their elected representatives, to retain some form of elected school governance. Where Blacks dissented from this position, it was out of frustration with an elected board that had governed ineffectively and ineptly and had failed to satisfactorily improve the education of Black youth. In both instances, education per se was held in the highest regard by Blacks of all classes. Indeed, those who would have abolished the elected school board appeared to rank education above political empowerment in this particular case.

It should also be noted that while Black internal differences were difficult to resolve in this matter, Mel King, a highly respected activist, was able to convene Black community leadership across social class lines in an effort to do so. No Black constituency appeared to be fully satisfied with the Boston School Committee; so this issue did not seem to be one that sorted out Blacks by class.

From all of this, one might draw at least two conclusions regarding Black social class: (1) these cases tend to confirm strong support among Blacks for public education, regardless of social class status; and (2) Black social class interests were not revealed in these two cases.

Finally, our Boston study indicates that Blacks in Boston are not quite sure whether they should fight fire with fire and meet force with force, which are symmetrical ways of dealing with difficulties, or whether they should use asymmetrical techniques, such as meeting physical force with soul force. Blacks in Boston demonstrated their flexibility when one Black School Committee member voted for a Latino candidate to be superintendent of schools while other Blacks were campaigning for Boston's first Black superintendent. Several Blacks also supported the mayor's proposal for an appointed rather than an elected school committee, although most Blacks favored the latter proposal. Whether these actions represented wise asymmetrical approaches to public policymaking or simply the inability of the Black community in Boston to achieve a united front is hard to say. An analysis of more case studies is needed before one can make a determination about the wisdom of the Black community in the use of specific social action methods.

Finally, we offer an opinion about leadership and decision-making in the Black community and how it differs from leadership and decision making in the White community. An error often committed by social scientists is to assume that behavior, customs, and social structures and processes in the Black community are imitations of those found in the White community. While Floyd Hunter recognized that the Black community is organized, he also assumed that it "follows rather closely the pattern of the larger community" (Hunter 1953:114). James Q. Wilson made a similar observation based on his study, *Negro Politics*. He said that "the most important single conclusion that emerges from a survey of [African American] politics in large northern cities is that . . . the structure and style of [Black] politics reflects the politics of the city as a whole. Politics for [African Americans], as for other ethnic groups . . . can be viewed as a set of 'learned responses' which [they] acquire from the distinctive political system of the city in which [they] live" (Wilson 1960:22).

We discovered in Boston that Black leadership emerges from a consensus process rather than from a bureaucratic structure, that the consensus process is decentralized into spheres of influence, that Black community leaders in one sphere may not be leaders in another sphere, and that leadership in any sphere may change rapidly as a new consensus emerges regarding who should lead.

This method of selecting and sustaining community leaders is significantly different from the hierarchical structure of leadership found in the White community. It is a method of selecting and sustaining leaders that is uniquely characteristic of subdominant people of power. It is a mistake to recognize the method of choosing leaders in the Black community as an imitation of the way leaders are chosen in the White community. Much misunderstanding has resulted from this mistake that is manifested in the writings of Floyd Hunter, James Q. Wilson, and others.

Our study indicates that more research is needed that seeks to discover the significant ways in which leadership and decision making in subdominant populations differ from those found among dominant people of power, and also how these different decision-making practices complement each other.

REFERENCES

Ardrey, Robert. 1966. *The Territorial Imperative*. New York: Atheneum.

Dahl, Robert. 1961. *Who Governs?* New Haven, CT: Yale University Press.

Hunter, Floyd. 1953. *Community Power Structure*. Chapel Hill: University of North Carolina Press.

King, Martin Luther, Jr. 1958. *Stride Toward Freedom*. New York: Harper and Row.

King, Martin Luther, Jr. 1967. *Where Do We Go from Here, Chaos or Community?* Boston: Beacon Press.

Miller, William R. 1968. *Martin Luther King, Jr.: His Life, Martyrdom, and Meaning for the World*. New York: Avon.

Oates, Stephen. 1982. *Let the Trumpet Sound: The Life of Martin Luther King, Jr.* New York: Mentor Book of the New American Library.

Peterson, Paul. 1981. *City Limits*. Chicago: University of Chicago Press.

Warren, Roland L. 1963. *The Community in America*. Chicago: Rand McNally.

Wilson, James Q. 1960. *Negro Politics*. New York: The Free Press.

For Further Reading

Aberback, Joel D., and Jack Walker. 1973. *Race in the City*. Boston: Little, Brown and Co.

Alexander, Jeffrey C., Bernhard Giesen, Richard Münch, and Neil J. Smelser, eds., 1987. *The Micro-Macro Link*. Berkeley, CA: University of California Press.

Altshuler, Alan A. *Community Control: The Black Demand for Participation in Large American Cities*. Indianapolis: Bobbs-Merrill.

Ashline, Nelson, Thomas R. Pezzullo, and Charles I. Norris, eds. 1976. *Education, Inequality and National Policy*. Lexington, MA: Lexington Books.

Axelrod, Robert. 1970. *Conflict of Interest*. Chicago: Markham.

Blackwell, James E. 1975. *The Black Community*. New York: Dodd, Mead and Co.

Blackwell, James E., and Philip Hart. 1982. *Cities, Suburbs and Blacks*. Dix Hills, NY: General Hall.

Boudon, Raymond. 1979. *The Logic of Social Action*. Boston: Routledge and Kegan Paul.

Bredenmeier, Mary E., and Harry C. Bredenmeier. 1978. *Social Forces in Education*. Sherman Oaks, CA: Alfred Publishing Co.

Castells, Manuel. 1983. *The City and the Grassroots*. Berkeley, CA: University of California Press.

Comer, James P. 1972. *Beyond Black and White*. New York: Quadrangel Books.

Cookson, Peter, Jr. 1994. *School Choice*. New Haven, CT: Yale University Press.

Corson, David, and Sylvie Lemay. 1996. *Social Justice and Language Policy*. Toronto, Ontario: Oise Press.

Crain, Robert L. 1968. *The Politics of School Desegregation*. Chicago: Aldine.

Crain, Robert L., R. Mahard, and R. E. Narot. 1982. *Making Desegregation Work*. Cambridge, MA: Ballinger Publishing Co.

Cross, Theodore. 1984. *The Black Power Imperative*. New York: Faulkner.

Dahl, Robert A. 1961. *Who Governs?* New Haven, CT: Yale University Press.

Dahl, Robert A. 1967. *Pluralist Democracy in the United States*. Chicago: Rand McNally and Co.

Dahl, Robert A. 1981. *Democracy in the United States*. Dallas: Houghton Mifflin Co.

Dawson, Michael. 1994. *Behind the Mule, Race and Class in African-American Politics*. Princeton. NJ: Princeton University Press.

Dentler, Robert A., and Anne L. Hafner. 1997. *Hosting Newcomers*. New York: Teachers College Press.

Dentler, Robert, and Marvin B. Scott. 1981. *Schools on Trial*. Cambridge, MA: Abt Books.

Dunham, Arthur. 1970. *The New Community Organization*. New York: Cromwell Co.

Enloe, Cynthia. 1973. *Ethnic Conflict and Political Development*. Boston: Little, Brown and Co.

Epps, Edgar, ed. 1973. *Race Relations*. Cambridge, MA: Winthrop Publishers.

Feagin, Joe. 1995. *White Racism*. New York: Routledge.

Fischer, Claude, Michael Haut, Martin Sanchez Jankowski, Samuel R. Lucas, Ann Swidler, and Kim Voss. 1996. *Inequality by Design*. Princeton, NJ: Princeton University Press.

Fiske, Edward B. 1991. *Smart Schools, Smart Kids*. New York: Simon and Schuster.

Formisano, Ronald P. 1991. *Boston Against Busing*. Chapel Hill, NC: University of North Carolina Press.

Frederickson, George M. 1981. *White Supremacy*. New York: Oxford University.

Freire, Paulo. 1985. *The Politics of Education*. Grandby, MA: Bergin and Garvey Publishers.

Gamson, William A. 1968. *Power and Discontent*. Homewood, IL: Dorsey Press.

Gamson, William A. 1975. *The Strategy of Protest*. Chicago: Dorsey Press.

Graham, Hugh Davis. 1990. *The Civil Rights Era*. New York: Oxford University Press.

Gutierrez, Gustavo. 1983. *The Power of the Poor in History*. Mary Knoll, NY: Orbis.

Hacker, Andrew. 1992. *Two Nations*. New York: Charles Scribner's Sons.

Heifetz, Ronald A. 1994. *Leadership without Easy Answers*. Cambridge, MA: Harvard University Press.

Higginbotham, A. Leon, Jr. 1978. *In the Matter of Color*. New York: Oxford University Press.

Hochschild, Jennifer. 1984. *The New American Dilemma*. New Haven, CT: Yale University Press.

Hillery, George A., Jr. 1967. *Communal Organizations*. Chicago: University of Chicago Press.

Hunt, Chester L., and Lewis Walker. 1979. *Ethnic Dynamics*. Holmes Beach, FL: Learning Publications.

Katz, Neil, and John W. Lawyer. 1993. *Conflict Resolution*. Thousand Oaks, CA: Corwin Press.

Katzman, Martin. 1971. *The Political Economy of Urban Schools*. Cambridge, MA: Harvard University Press.

Kochman, Thomas. 1981. *Black and White Styles in Conflict*. Chicago: University of Chicago Press.

Kriesberg, Louis. 1982. *Social Conflict*. Englewood Cliffs, NJ: Prentice-Hall.

Loevy, Robert D., ed. 1997. *The Civil Rights Act of 1964*. Albany, NY: State University Press of New York.

Lunenburg, Fred C., and Allan Ornstein. 1991. *Educational Administration*, Belmont, CA: Wadsworth.

MacIver, R. M. 1947. *The Web of Government*. New York: Macmillan.

Maxwell, Gerald, and Pamela Oliver. 1993. *The Critical Mass in Collective Action*. New York: Cambridge University Press.

Mayhew, Leon H. 1968. *Law and Equal Opportunity*. Cambridge, MA: Harvard University Press.

McDougal, Harold A. 1993. *Baltimore, A Theory of Community*. Philadelphia: Temple University Press.

McKelvey, Charles. 1994. *The African-American Movement*. Dix Hills, NY: General Hall.

Newman, Dorothy, Nancy J. Amide, Barbara L. Carter, Dawn Day, William J. Kruvant, and Jack S. Russell. 1978. *Protest, Politics, and Prosperity*. New York: Pantheon.

Oliver, Melvin, and Thomas Shapiro. 1995. *Black Wealth/White Wealth*. New York: Routledge.

Orfield, Gary, and Susan Eaton. 1996. *Dismantling Desegregation*. New York: The New Press.

Paul, Arnold M., ed. 1972. *Black Americans and the Supreme Court since Emancipation*. New York: Holt, Rinehart and Winston.

Piore, Michael J. 1995. *Beyond Individualism*. Cambridge, MA: Harvard University Press.

Polsby, Nelson W. 1963. *Community Power and Political Theory*. New Haven, CT: Yale University Press.

Rendon, Laura I., and Richard O. Hope. 1996. *Educating a New Majority*. San Francisco: Jossey-Bass.

Rose, Mike. 1989. *Lives on the Boundary*. New York: Penguin Books.

Rothstein, Stanley W. 1991. *Identity and Ideology, Sociocultural Theories of Schooling*. Westport, CT: Greenwood Press.

Seeley, David. 1981. *Education Through Partnership*. Cambridge, MA: Ballinger.

Smith, Robert C. 1995. *Racism in the Post-Civil Rights Era*. Albany, NY: State University of New York Press.

Steinberg, James B., et al. 1992. *Urban America*. Santa Monica, CA: Rand.

Swain, Carol M. 1993. *Blackfaces, Black Interests*. Cambridge, MA: Harvard University Press.

Terkel, Studs. 1992. *Race, How Blacks and Whites Think and Feel about the American Obsession*. New York: The New Press.

Thomas, Gail E., ed. 1990. *U.S. Race Relations in the 1980s and 1990s*. New York: Hemisphere Publishing Corp.

Weinberg, Meyer, ed. 1968. *Integrated Education*. Beverly Hills, CA: Glencoe Press.

Weinberg, Meyer. 1981. *The Education of Poor and Minority Children*. 2 vols. Westport, CT: Greenwood Press.

Wharf, Brian, and Michael Clague. 1977. *Community Organizing*. New York: Oxford University Press.

Whitmier, Claude, ed. 1993. *In the Company of Others*. New York: Putnam.

Wileden, Arthur F. 1970. *Community Development*. Totowa, NJ: Bedminster Press.

Williams, Robin M., Jr., and Margaret W. Ryan. 1954. *Schools in Transition*. Chapel Hill, NC: University of North Carolina.

Willie, Charles V. 1978. *The Sociology of Urban Education, Desegregation and Integration*. Westport, CT: Praeger.

Willie, Charles V. 1983. *Race, Ethnicity and Socioeconomic Status*. Dix Hills, NY: General Hall.

Willie, Charles V. 1984. *School Desegregation Plans that Work*. Westport, CT: Greenwood Press.

Willie, Charles V. 1987. *Effective Education*. Westport, CT: Greenwood Press.

Willie, Charles V. 1994. *Theories of Human Social Action*. Dix Hills, NY: General Hall.

Willie, Charles V., ed. 1977. *Black/Brown/White Relations*. New Brunswick, NJ: Transaction Books.

Willie, Charles V., and Michael Alves. 1996. *Controlled Choice*. Providence, RI: New England Desegregation Assistance Center at Brown University.

Willie, Charles V., with Jerome Beker. 1973. *Race Mixing in the Public Schools*. Westport, CT: Praeger.

Willie, Charles V., Antoine Garibaldi, and Wornie Reed, eds. 1991. *The Education of African-Americans*. Westport, CT: Auburn House.

Willie, Charles V., and Susan Greenblatt. 1981. *Community Politics and Educational Change*. New York: Longman.

Zinn, Howard. 1995. *A People's History of the United States—1492–present*. New York: Harper Perennial.

Index

About the Authors

RALPH EDWARDS is Senior Research Associate at the Center for Innovation in Urban Education at Northeastern University. Edwards was an elementary school principal in Harlem for ten years and Assistant Professor of Education at Boston College prior to his current research activities.

CHARLES V. WILLIE is Professor of Education and Urban Studies, Graduate School of Education, Harvard University. Willie has served as a community planner, university administrator as well as a court-appointed Master in *Morgan v. Hennigan* (1974). Among his earlier publications are *School Desegregation Plans That Work* (Greenwood, 1984) and *Effective Education* (Greenwood, 1988).

ISBN 0-275-96201-6

90000>

9 780275 962012

EAN

HARDCOVER BAR CODE